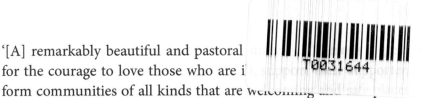

STRUGGLING WITH GOD

Christopher C. H. Cook is Emeritus Professor in the Institute for Medical Humanities at Durham University. He is Chair of the Spirituality & Psychiatry Special Interest Group at the Royal College of Psychiatrists and Honorary Chaplain for Tees, Esk & Wear Valleys NHS Foundation Trust. He was awarded the Canterbury Cross by the Archbishop of Canterbury in 2020 for his work on theology and psychiatry, and the Oskar Pfister Award by the American Psychiatric Association in 2021 for his work on religion and psychiatry. His books include *Hearing Voices, Demonic and Divine* (2018) and *Christians Hearing Voices* (2020).

Isabelle Hamley is a writer, theologian and speaker. She is currently working as Theological Adviser to the House of Bishops, after posts as Chaplain to the Archbishop of Canterbury, parish priest, university chaplain and theology tutor. Before ordination she was a probation officer. She is passionate about the Old Testament and the importance of Scripture to the life of the Church and has written in particular on the Bible and mental health, and on matters of justice, violence and faith.

John Swinton is Professor in Practical Theology and Pastoral Care and Chair in Divinity and Religious Studies at the University of Aberdeen. He previously worked as a registered mental health nurse, and then as a mental health chaplain in both hospital and community. In 2004, he founded the University of Aberdeen's Centre for Spirituality, Health and Disability. He has published widely within the areas of mental health, dementia, disability theology, spirituality and healthcare, and pastoral care. His previous books include *Dementia: Living in the memories of God* (2012) and *Finding Jesus in the Storm* (2020).

STRUGGLING WITH GOD

Mental health and Christian spirituality

Christopher C. H. Cook, Isabelle Hamley and John Swinton

that only other soldiers who have been alongside them in battle truly understand what they went through. The same is true of many jobs and experiences. They create a fellowship of suffering or celebration that is one of a kind. It is both natural and necessary in order to find support or to rejoice.

However, if the compartments become too separate then there is often a breakdown of ability to relate and even of general wellbeing. Isolation results in mental, emotional, spiritual and physical harm. One of the early and too-often-forgotten prisoners of the South African apartheid regime was Professor Robert Sobukwe, founder of the Pan Africanist Congress. He was held for over eight years in the most stringent solitary confinement, and in the end it wore down even this exceptionally brave man's health in every way until he died. Community, the breaking down of isolation in every part of life, is a significant therapeutic aid in recovering from diseases of all kinds.

Human beings are not Lego toys, made up of free-standing and differently shaped bricks. They are the most remarkable beings, in which everything is connected to everything, interacting in ways far beyond any adequate analysis. Humans work on intangibles such as loving relationships and acceptance, tangibles such as food, water and shelter, and contexts of security or good air, or balanced diets, or fulfilling work and supportive communities.

The remarkable form of this book is, in the context of mental health, to bring together a holistic spiritual approach relating to sufferers, those who love them, and the challenge of the response needed from churches. It is a book of loving approaches to mental health – founded spiritually in the love of Christ – in its analysis, in its attitudes and in its proposed activities. It remembers the body as well as the mind, the history and the context.

Its three authors demonstrate in this book how partnerships overcome compartmentalization. Christopher Cook is a psychiatrist and priest. John Swinton is a theologian who has spent a lifetime developing theological thinking on disability and mental illness. Isabelle Hamley (who worked with me as Chaplain) is a biblical scholar and experienced pastor. They together respond to the gap between necessary specialized thinking and knowledge on the one hand, and on the other the reality

Introduction

Jesus came alongside people struggling with their mental and physical health. Take, for example, the woman in Luke's Gospel who had struggled for 18 years with a condition which caused her to be 'bent over' so that she could not stand upright (Luke 13.10–17). Luke tells us that she was afflicted by a 'spirit of weakness',[1] but Jesus does not cast out any evil spirits; he simply calls her over and says, 'Woman, you are set free from your ailment.'[2] He lays his hands on her, and she stands upright and praises God. In this brief story we see Jesus come alongside a woman who is struggling physically, emotionally and spiritually. He notices her, he calls to her, and he sets her free.

This does not please the leader of the synagogue, who appears more concerned with his interpretation of what is permissible in Scripture than he is about the suffering of the woman. He is prejudiced by his own religious world view and does not see the power of God at work in the life of this woman in her need. He stigmatizes her, reducing her identity to that of a case of religious law-breaking. Jesus, in contrast, lifts her up, calling her a 'daughter of Abraham', and sets her free.

Many today are struggling, physically, emotionally and spiritually. Perhaps you are one of them? Or maybe someone you know and love is struggling? In this book we will be focusing particularly on mental and spiritual struggles, but human beings have bodies and – like the woman in Luke's Gospel – our wellbeing is about physical, mental and spiritual health in harmony. Like Jesus, we need to see the needs of the whole person, lifting people up in our prayers and in health and pastoral

---

1 English translations of v. 11 vary widely, including 'spirit of infirmity' (KJV), 'crippled by a spirit' (NIV) and 'disabling spirit' (ESV), but 'spirit of weakness' provides a good literal translation of the Greek.

2 Here and elsewhere, all English translations are taken from the New Revised Standard Version (NRSV), Anglicized edition, unless stated otherwise.

care, and not reducing them by way of prejudice and stigma within our churches or wider society.

I (Chris) am left wondering how many times this daughter of Abraham must have prayed for healing and found none. Did she feel deserted by God? Was she blamed for her own suffering by others, as Job was? (See Chapter 2.) Did the physical, emotional and spiritual struggle sometimes seem just too much to bear? Whether or not this was the case, in the eyes of others before Jesus meets her, this woman appears excluded, diminished and weighed down. When Jesus calls her a daughter of Abraham, we have a glimpse into her true identity. She is chosen, loved and faithful, a recipient of God's promises.

Not every story of struggle and suffering has such a happy ending in either Scripture or our experience. However, we cannot imagine any situation of this kind in which Jesus is unconcerned. If he seems absent, then perhaps we have only come into the story halfway through – during the equivalent of this woman's 18 years of struggle. Or perhaps – in order to truly understand feelings of God's absence – we have to fast-forward to that later part of the Gospel story where Jesus cries from the cross that he himself feels abandoned by God? Whether in a dramatic healing, or in struggling for 18 years without any seeming answer, prayer on the road to recovery from mental health problems is about finding God with us in the struggle – though that may in itself be a struggle!

At least one in five, and in some parts of the world perhaps as many as one in two, people experience mental ill health during the course of their lifetime. This means that mental health is everyone's concern. If we have not had our own mental health problems, then we certainly know others who have. They are among our family and friends; they are colleagues at work, and members of the same church congregation. If we have not noticed this, then it may be because they have not felt able to talk to us about their struggles. There is a stigma attached to mental ill health which makes people feel, like the woman in Luke's Gospel, that they are less than they should be. Mental ill health leads to exclusion, prejudice and shame. Consequently, it is difficult to talk about, not least within a Christian community that may emphasize God's offer of abundant life. If my life doesn't feel very abundant, perhaps God has forgotten me, or maybe my faith is not all that it should be?

What do we mean by mental health?

The concept of mental health is explored in more depth in Chapter 1, but it is important to clarify some things at the outset. First, mental health can mean very different things to different people. On the one hand, it is about human flourishing – mental wellbeing. On the other hand, it often refers in practice to exactly the opposite – mental illness. Both meanings will be discussed in this book, but we are mainly concerned here with the latter – with the struggles that people have when they are having a problem with their mental health. These problems may or may not be associated with a diagnosis, and mental health professionals may or may not have been involved, but either way they are a cause for concern. People are often afraid of going to see a mental health professional, for fear of what they will say or do, and for fear of the stigma that this might attract.

Second, very different kinds of language are used to talk about mental health. The language most widely used for understanding mental health problems in the Western world is the language of medicine. Mental health problems are understood as illnesses, or disorders, and are treated by doctors, nurses and other mental health professionals within a system of healthcare. As will be explored later in the book, this has its advantages and disadvantages. In general, we treat people who are sick with compassion, we do not usually blame them for being ill, and we offer the resources of medicine to help them recover. It is also true that virtually every illness has physical, psychological and social dimensions, whether the diagnosis is one of depression, cancer or Covid-19. Understanding mental illness in this context has brought great advances in treatment, and a generally much more supportive and sympathetic response from society.

Notwithstanding the benefits of a medical approach to mental health care, mental illnesses are not quite like other illnesses, and they are associated with significant stigma, prejudice and misunderstanding in a way that most other illnesses are not. The medicalization of mental health care has also removed it – to a large extent – from the world of spiritual and pastoral care. This has led to a disintegration of care, so that care of the human spirit is not seen (as it properly should be) as inseparable from the care of mind and body, and of the individual in relationship with God and others. It is therefore important to explore different models of understanding and also, without dismissing the value of a medical approach, sometimes to use different language. For example, in Chapters 4 and 5, in the context of thinking about recovery and disability respectively, the language of 'mental health challenges' will be used. However, we need to be careful that this term does not simply become a way of perpetuating the stigma associated with the concept of mental illness.

Whatever language we use, mental illness or mental health challenges, we are talking here about human experiences which can feel like a real struggle – a struggle within, a struggle with others and perhaps even a struggle with God. The good news is that God, in Jesus, comes alongside us in our struggle and transforms what can seem like a struggle with (against) God into a struggle with (alongside) God.

What is this book about?

This book is for those who struggle, for those who come alongside those who struggle and for those who would like to come alongside but fear that they might do or say the wrong thing. It aims to be informative, but also to facilitate spiritual and prayerful reflection. It is about mental health and, in particular, mental illness (or mental health challenges). It is not primarily about mental wellbeing, although inevitably we do discuss this as well. This book is not about intellectual disability (or learning disability), and it is not about neurodiversity (or neurodivergence). We shall thus not be discussing topics such as autism, attention deficit hyperactivity disorder (ADHD) or dyslexia.

In the first chapter of the book, we will drill down in more depth on the relationship between spiritual and mental health. A brief introduction to the different kinds of mental illness is provided and, correspondingly, the different kinds of spiritual struggle that they represent. Attention is given, among other things, to anxiety and affective disorders, eating disorders, personality disorders, dementia and psychosis. Prayer is the Christian context within which such struggles with mental health are worked out.

In Chapter 2, we explore the association of mental illness with stigma, looking at how it arises and how it is expressed. Stigma is a 'spoiled' human identity. In the Gospels, we discover that Jesus welcomes people regardless of what others think about them and offers a new way of relating within which human identity is not constrained by the complexity of the things with which we struggle. Sadly, this is not always appreciated within our churches, and God and the community of faith can sometimes seem to be a part of the problem rather than the solution.

In Chapter 3, attention is given to the concept of resilience. Medical and psychological research demonstrates that spirituality and faith provide important coping resources in the face of illness and adversity. This chapter explores the ways in which these resources may be drawn upon by Christians struggling with mental health problems. The concept of 'spiritual struggles' is examined – looking at the helpful and unhelpful ways in which Christians cope psychologically and spiritually with mental health problems. Christians can faithfully respond to struggles with their mental health, knowing that God is with them in their struggles.

In Chapter 4, the concept of recovery – currently seen as very important within mental health services – is explored from a Christian perspective. Particular attention is given here to the ways in which Christians struggling with mental health challenges may recover in the context of a loving Christian community. Healing, recovery and wellbeing do not necessarily entail the elimination of suffering, but rather finding God, and struggling with God, in the midst of mental health challenges.

Mental health problems represent the leading cause of disability worldwide, but the relationship between mental health challenges and disability is complex and contentious. In Chapter 5, the disability associated with mental health challenges is considered within the broader context of Christian thinking about disability. Christians struggling with the limits imposed by anxiety, depression and other chronic mental health challenges can find themselves disabled by church communities and Christian theologies. In interpretation of Scripture, and in our approach to prayer and worship together, we all need to be much more attentive to members of the Church who are struggling with mental health challenges.

The final chapter of the book addresses mental health in relation to the mission of the Church. The churches have an important part to play in combating stigma, in providing a loving welcome to people struggling with mental health issues, and in helping Christians to draw on the resources of their faith in coping with illness, anxiety and adversity. Some pointers are offered to ways in which churches can fulfil this role more effectively in practice.

Throughout the book we have drawn on biblical insights, the lived experience of those who struggle with mental health challenges, the insights of psychiatry and the mental health sciences, and the resources of theology. Weaving together these different strands of thinking, we have sought to provide a biblical and prayerful approach to the topic which is sensitive to the very real struggles that many of us face as Christians. You may be reading this as someone who is struggling with your own mental health challenges, or as someone who cares for a friend or family member who is struggling. Either way, we hope that this book will help you to find God amid the struggle. Each chapter concludes with a biblical reflection, a prayer, some questions for further discussion and resources for further reading.

1

Christian spirituality and mental health

Spirituality is seen by some as being the opposite of religion (including Christianity). Spirituality is – they say – full of life, and free from rules, institutions and hierarchies. In our very individualistic society, the freedom to define one's own spirituality can seem very attractive. Christian spirituality, in contrast, is portrayed as 'one size fits all', restricting and outmoded. That it is possible to present things in this way might suggest that Christians haven't done a very good job at promoting the 'good news' that is at the heart of their faith. But what is this good news? And what does an authentic 'Christian' spirituality look like?

In this book, we want to argue that Christianity is good news for mental health. We do not imagine that human beings have bodies, minds and souls that are all separate pieces – plugged together like Lego bricks but nonetheless different parts. To be human, to be a whole person, is to be a bodily, social, psychological and spiritual unity. To be a Christian is to look to Jesus as the model of what being a whole person is all about. We have got used to thinking that Jesus was a spiritual teacher and that mental health is something that belongs to medical professionals, and that the two are quite different. While there might be some truth in this, we have created too much of a gulf between the two. Spiritual and mental wellbeing are all a part of the same picture of human flourishing, and Jesus' life and teaching reflected that.

Take Jesus' teaching on worry, for example: 'Therefore I tell you, do not worry about your life, what you will eat or what you will drink, or about your body, what you will wear. Is not life more than food, and the body more than clothing?' (Matthew 6.25). Too often, this verse has been used to make people feel guilty for worrying. So, someone who is struggling with anxiety then ends up struggling with anxiety *and* guilt. Let's call this person Susan, and let's say she is worried about losing her job, or about a diagnosis of cancer. Susan talks to a Christian friend, or perhaps a pastor or priest, about her problems, and this verse is used to 'comfort' her. She does not need to worry! Unfortunately, human beings do not have an inbuilt worry switch which can be used to turn off the worry. We can't simply choose not to worry. Nor can we choose not to feel guilty about the fact that we are worrying – so Susan ends up worried and guilty rather than just worried.

Actually, if we look at this verse in the wider context of the Sermon on the Mount, we discover that it is a part of Jesus' teaching on prayer. We discover (in Matthew 6.32) that Jesus affirms the fact that God – our heavenly Father – knows that we need these things. The problem is not that we worry about these things, but that we don't worry about even more important things. At the heart of the sermon is Jesus' teaching on prayer, including the prayer that we know as the Lord's Prayer, in which we are encouraged to ask for 'our daily bread'. So, Jesus is not telling us that food and clothing, jobs and families, do not matter. He is, rather, asking us to get things in perspective. We worry about the things that matter to us. Do we worry about God's kingdom? If not, why not? The first things to ask for, the things that matter most, are that God's kingdom may come and that his will be done.

This is, of course, not easy, and we find Jesus later, in Gethsemane, struggling with it himself. Grieved and agitated, he prays: 'My Father, if it is possible, let this cup pass from me; yet not what I want but what you want' (Matthew 26.39).

Christian life is therefore not easy, for it is about following Jesus' example. Like Jesus, we can find that it is a struggle, but it is about finding that our struggles – our worries and anxieties – get put properly into context in our relationship with God. In a very real sense, Christian spirituality is about struggling *with* God. That is, finding that God is alongside us in our struggles. However, it can also feel, as it did for Jacob, that we are struggling with God in a different sense – wrestling with him:

Jacob was left alone; and a man wrestled with him until daybreak. When the man saw that he did not prevail against Jacob, he struck him on the hip socket; and Jacob's hip was put out of joint as he

wrestled with him. Then he said, 'Let me go, for the day is breaking.' But Jacob said, 'I will not let you go, unless you bless me.' So he said to him, 'What is your name?' And he said, 'Jacob.' Then the man said, 'You shall no longer be called Jacob, but Israel, for you have striven with God and with humans, and have prevailed.'
(Genesis 32.24–28)

Christian spirituality

Spirituality is a popular concept today, but eludes any precise or agreed definition. It is usually taken to be concerned with relationships, and particularly relationship with 'something greater' (whether or not conceived of as God) and with meaning and purpose in life. For Christians, relationship with God is understood in the light of the life and death of Jesus. We might say that Christian spirituality is a participation in the life, death and resurrection of Jesus. This is about living life, as St Paul says, 'in Christ'; it is about modelling our lives on Jesus' life, and Jesus' life was a life of prayer.

Prayer is not just about words. Although the Lord's Prayer has come down to us as a form of words, it is found in the middle of the teaching that we know as the Sermon on the Mount. In this sermon, Jesus talks about letting our good works be like a light that causes others to praise God; he talks about commandments and righteousness, about being angry, about forgiving others, sexual attraction, loving enemies as well as neighbours, and giving to the poor. His sermon is about the things that we worry over, the things that matter to us, and how we deal with these anxieties.

Since the earliest days of the Church, Christians have made prayer a priority. Living as hermits in the desert, gathering in communities dedicated to prayer, and engaging in social action, Christians have explored almost every conceivable way of using human minds and bodies to pray. Speech and silence, meditation, imagination and contemplation, pilgrimage, dance, song, ritual, art, incense, architecture, nature, fasting, self-discipline and self-denial, time and seasons – all these have been enlisted as aids to prayer. This diversity of practices in prayer finds expression in a range of different Christian spiritual traditions. For example, the early desert fathers and mothers subjected themselves to lives of physical discipline and self-denial in order that they might be able to devote themselves better to prayer. The spiritual exercises of St Ignatius make extensive use of imaginative meditation on Scripture. Contemporary Charismatic spirituality makes colourful use of music, song and dance.

If Christianity is 'one size fits all', then that may only be because it is inclusive of diversity – diversity of people and diversity of the forms which Christian spirituality has taken throughout history and in different cultures and contexts. Yet, in all of this diversity, we find a central concern of giving attention to God, and thus to God's involvement in his world. Simone Weil, in *Gravity and Grace*, suggested – somewhat provocatively – that: 'Attention, taken to its highest degree, is the same thing as prayer. It presupposes faith and love. Absolutely unmixed attention is prayer' (Weil, 1952, p. 105).

Now, we might wonder what taking attention to its 'highest degree' might be. In Luke's Gospel, in Jesus' parable, the prodigal son gives his attention to all of the wrong things before realizing that his attention should be focused differently, at which point he returns to his father. Likewise, in the story of the good Samaritan, also in Luke's Gospel, the priest and the Levite, as well as the Samaritan, attend to the man who has fallen victim to thieves, but the priest and the Levite do so only in order to cross the road and avoid getting involved. Their attention is mis-directed. The Samaritan gives proper attention to a neighbour in need and takes action. In Matthew's Gospel (25.31–46), we discover that it is in giving attention to the hungry, the thirsty, the stranger, those who are naked, sick or in prison that we give attention to Christ.

Mental health

According to the World Health Organization (WHO), mental health is 'a state of mental well-being that enables people to cope with the stresses of life, realize their abilities, learn well and work well, and contribute to their community'.[3]

---

3 <www.who.int/news-room/fact-sheets/detail/mental-health-strengthening-our-response> (accessed 23 December 2022).

There are limitations to this definition. For example, it says nothing about family, and it presumes that work might be available. What of the mental health of the unemployed? It also says nothing about spirituality. However, it is helpful in reminding us that mental health is not about the absence of symptoms of mental disorder. It is about whether and how we are able to deal with the challenges in life; it is about relationships; it is about how we contribute to the community. It is – we might say – about our sense of vocation.

Much could be said about Christian vocation, which may take many forms, but – as suggested above – all Christians have a vocation to pray. We might, therefore, suggest that for Christians mental health is about fulfilling our vocations in God's kingdom. Whatever our vocation may be, and however unique it may be, as a Christian it will be a vocation to pray. Our prayer may be lived out as a nurse, a teacher, a builder, a pastor, or in countless other ways, but for the Christian prayer will involve every area of life, not least those central concerns that find expression in the priorities that express themselves in our use of time.

This understanding of mental health as concerned with vocation is fundamentally about relationship. First, it is about relationship with ourselves: our thoughts and feelings, our appetites and desires, our memories and imagination, our behaviour in the world. Second, it is about relationship with others. Most importantly, it is about relationship with God. As we are reminded in Matthew 25, these relationships are not independent of one another. Knowing what it is to be hungry should influence the way in which I see my hungry neighbour, and my response to my neighbour is in turn a reflection of my relationship with God.

This broad view of mental health is something that concerns us all; it is about a positive sense of how well we can respond to the physical, mental and spiritual challenges that life presents. However, it is also concerned with those particular conditions that we refer to as mental illnesses or mental disorders.

Mental illness

Mental illness may take many different forms. It is concerned with the ways in which our thoughts and feelings, appetites, mental faculties, sense experiences and behaviours sometimes seem to malfunction. They do the wrong thing at the wrong time, or they stop working, or they are exaggerated or distorted in some way. We get anxious when there is no reason to be anxious, or we hear distressing voices even when there is no one there. Or perhaps we have a distorted body image, or we find that our mood swings from high to low and back again. Or perhaps we find ourselves doing things that we wish we wouldn't – drinking too much alcohol, or constantly washing our hands.

Reference to these concerns as illnesses relies upon an extended metaphor. We treat the anxiety, or depression, or hand-washing, as a 'symptom' of an underlying 'illness'. However, in most cases, we don't have any clear underlying pathology that can be seen under a micro-scope, or on an X-ray or MRI scan, or measured in a test tube. There are some exceptions to this. For example, we now know quite a lot about the brain pathology that underlies dementia; we can detect changes in the brain which are visible under the microscope (post-mortem) and on brain scans (during life). We also know quite a lot about the genetic predisposition to a range of different mental illnesses, although the precise genetic changes are difficult to pin down. We have some evidence that there are probably changes to brain chemistry in depression. Despite this, in most cases, mental illnesses are diagnosed on the basis of signs and symptoms, such as anxiety, hallucinations or impaired memory, not blood tests or known causes.

Mental illnesses, or mental disorders as they are also known, are therefore classified primarily on the basis of signs and symptoms. The two main systems of classifying and diagnosing these conditions are the *International Classification of Diseases of the World Health Organization*, now in its eleventh revision (ICD-11),[4] and the *Diagnostic and Statistical Manual of the American Psychiatric Association*, now in its fifth edition (DSM-5) (American Psychiatric Association, 2013). We will not go into the detail of these manuals here, but some of the major headings are as follows:

Schizophrenia, and other conditions known as primary 'psychoses';
Mood disorders;

---

4 <https://icd.who.int/en>.

Anxiety or fear-related disorders;
Disorders associated with stress or trauma;
Dissociative disorders;
Eating disorders;
Substance-related disorders and other addictions;
Personality disorders;
Neurocognitive disorders (including the dementias).

This is not a complete list (for example, it does not include developmental problems, or the diagnoses used in child and adolescent mental health services), but it covers most of the major diagnostic groups affecting adults. Each of these groups of conditions is associated with its own set of physical, psychological, social and spiritual challenges, but we will focus here on the spiritual. In what ways might someone suffering from one of these conditions find that he or she is struggling with God?

The concept of **psychosis** is controversial, difficult to define, associated with stigma (see Chapter 2) and confusing for people who are not mental health professionals. The term is sometimes now replaced by reference to 'major mental illness' (which is also not an ideal term, and not necessarily exactly the same thing). Despite this, psychosis has long been recognized as a major category of mental disorders and seems unlikely to disappear from use any time soon. It is said to be characterized by a loss of contact with reality. (Christians, and others, may well ask, 'What is reality?') In practice, this has generally meant experience of delusions and hallucinations, but delusions are also hard to define and it is now known that hallucinations, and other psychotic-like experiences, occur widely in the general population.

The title of Richard Dawkins' book *The God Delusion* notoriously implies that belief in God is delusional – non-rational, false and unshakeable – but Dawkins is not a mental health professional and does not show any interest in grappling with the core issues of mental health. Definitions of delusion used by psychiatrists and other mental health professionals explicitly exclude religious and other sociocul- turally affirmed beliefs. There is much in life, including many of the things that we value most, such as faith, hope and love, that cannot be proved scientifically. These things are not delusions. Nevertheless, most religious people immediately recognize strongly held beliefs that arise in the mind of someone suffering from a psychosis as outside the realm of what is normally accepted as a part of their faith. Believing that Jesus is the Son of God is one thing. Believing that I am Jesus is quite another. The problem is that in-between these clear-cut examples there are many shades of personally held beliefs that seem strange and irrational but may or may not be evidence of illness.

A similar problem arises with hallucinations. Generally speaking, hallucinations are perception-like experiences that arise in the absence of any objective stimulus in the real world. I might hear someone speaking when no one visible is there, or see something that others cannot see. These experiences are commonly distinguished (at least in the minds of the faithful) from religious visions, or from experiences of hearing God speak, but actually the form of the experience is in many ways similar, and we now know that many ordinary people have such experiences (religious or not) without being diagnosable as suffering from any mental illness.

So, the struggle for people suffering from psychosis, and for their families and friends, is about how we know what is real. How do we respond when we feel deeply convinced that God has revealed something to us, but others do not agree that this is from God? How do we distinguish between 'revelations' of this kind that are just simple and sincere mistakes, and those that are evidence of mental illness? Indeed, can we distinguish? A short answer might be that such experiences are often associated with other evidence of illness (e.g. disorders of movement, or of the form that thoughts take rather than just their content), but in real life the distinction is often not straightforward.

Among the more severe examples of psychosis is the illness known as **schizophrenia**. Schizophrenia affects about 1 in 100 people worldwide. It can take a variety of different forms, and there is a view that it is actually a group of conditions – the 'schizophrenias' – rather than a single illness. In its most severe form, schizophrenia is associated with bizarre delusions, distressing voices, disrupted patterns of thought, loss of motivation, and impaired ability to sustain work and family relationships. Although modern treatments have improved prognosis, and early treatment with antipsychotic medication seems to make a big difference to the outcome, the long-term outcome can still be poor. However, identifying the problem early does seem to help, and some people having an acute episode of illness that looks like schizophrenia go on to recover completely. For reasons that are still not fully understood, the prognosis seems to be much better in less developed countries. There is thus a paradox in that medical treatment is known to be effective and yet countries in which such treatments are not widely available generally demonstrate better outcomes. This may have something to do with the extent to which people suffering from the illness in these countries are better accepted and more integrated into their communities. If this is so, Christian churches have a key part to play in providing safe and accepting spaces within the community, within which stigma and marginalization are not allowed to operate. Equally, churches – or individual Christians – can sometimes be very stigmatizing and can make things worse.

Mood disorders may take a variety of forms. There may be just one episode in a lifetime, or episodes may recur more or less frequently. They may be very severe, including features of psychosis, or very mild. Bipolar affective disorder involves episodes of both high (elated) and low (depressed) moods. Depression more commonly occurs on its own, whether as a recurrent condition or as a single episode. The word 'depression' is somewhat problematic as it refers both to a symptom and to a diagnosis. It may also be very severe, or very mild. Depression is a common experience and, at one level, it is hard to imagine anyone in adult life never having experienced depression in some sense. As with most other psychiatric conditions, the crucial questions, the ones that turn a normal feature of life into a diagnosis, are concerned with the extent to which the symptom (depression) interferes with daily life and functioning.

People seem to have suffered from struggles of this kind for thousands of years. In the Bible, we find King Saul afflicted by mood swings (attributed to an 'evil spirit' sent by God) which some see as similar to those encountered in bipolar disorder (1 Samuel 16—19). Elijah, following his encounter with the priests of Baal, is depressed, feeling hopeless, and asks that he might die (1 Kings 19). Whether due to circumstances, or seemingly without cause (attributed to an evil spirit in the Old Testament, or disturbed neurochemistry today), fluctuations in mood present a real spiritual challenge. Can we continue to love and serve God even when we feel hopeless and despairing? Is our faith all about feeling good, or does it endure when we feel hopeless? People who are depressed typically find it difficult to continue believing in God, or else may believe that they are worthy only of God's judgement.

Anxiety disorders include a series of conditions that are manifested either as excessive anxiety or else as anxiety experienced in inappropriate situations. These include phobias, panic attacks, generalized anxiety and obsessive compulsive disorder (although this is not actually grouped with anxiety disorders in DSM-5 or ICD-11). Everyone feels anxious sometimes, and a key consideration here is the extent to which the anxiety occurs at the wrong time, or is excessive, so that it interferes with life. Anxiety includes both a bodily component (fast pulse, sweating, a churning feeling in the stomach, etc.) and a mental component (which we will refer to here simply as 'worry').

Anxiety, like depression, is a part of everyone's life at some time or another. Generally speaking, we worry (or feel anxious) about the things that matter to us. Although we can learn to manage anxiety, this is not something that we can simply switch on and off. It is therefore a cause of concern to some Christians that Jesus appears to ask us to do the very thing that we cannot do and urges us not to worry. As discussed above, the things that we worry about say a lot about our priorities. However, we may find ourselves feeling anxious for no obvious reason. Like physical pain, anxiety can tell us that something is wrong, but it may not always point directly to the underlying cause.

There has been considerable interest in recent years in **trauma-related conditions**. The diagnosis of post-traumatic stress disorder (PTSD) was originally introduced in relation to combat-related stress, following the war in Vietnam. It is now understood as occurring much more widely, following exposure to any extreme or life-threatening event, and may include symptoms such as flashbacks, avoidance of reminders of the event, and hypervigilance. Complex PTSD (in ICD-11, but not included in DSM-5) occurs in relation to repeated or prolonged trauma, as for example in the case of childhood sexual abuse or domestic violence. Some therapists see 'trauma disorder' as a much wider category than is currently acknowledged in either DSM-5 or ICD-11.

The spiritual struggles associated with trauma-related conditions are diverse and considerable. In extreme circumstances people (such as soldiers in combat or healthcare workers amid a pandemic) can find themselves facing awful decisions (who lives and who dies?) and/or may have to make such decisions in the space of a few seconds. The regrets that follow may last a lifetime. Research is now focusing on the phenomenon of so-called 'moral injury', in which people find themselves distressed at having perpetrated, witnessed or failed to prevent actions which transgress their deeply held beliefs.

Within the life of the Church and wider society we are now more aware than ever before of the extent to which childhood sexual abuse has left women and men struggling into adult life with the psychological (and physical) wounds caused by abuse perpetrated on them when they were young. Where this abuse was perpetrated by clergy, or other church leaders, or by parents who espoused Christian faith, the spiritual consequences for survivors can be far-reaching. Anger with God, distrust of spiritual authority, doubt, loss of faith, and a host of other spiritual struggles may take many years to work through.

All of this can seem far from what we imagine Christian life should be all about, and yet the Bible contains many stories of trauma and survival, and does not shy away from reflecting on the spiritual struggles that ensue. The books of Jeremiah and Ezekiel address the context of a nation in exile, where people question why God has apparently failed to defend them from defeat and disaster in war. In the book of Judges, an unnamed woman is raped repeatedly until she dies. In Matthew's Gospel, Herod orders the mass slaughter of innocent children. God is portrayed in the Old and New Testaments as intimately concerned with trauma and suffering, not least in the person of Jesus, who was falsely condemned, beaten, and tortured to death. Perhaps one of the most astounding, and yet least talked-about, aspects of the resurrection is that the risen Christ apparently carries none of the psychological sequelae of the brutality inflicted on Jesus in his humanity.

Dissociative disorders include (among other diagnoses) dissociative identity disorder (DID, previously known as multiple personality disorder) and possession trance disorder, both of which have been associated with religious concerns about demon possession. However, dissociation is a widely experienced condition (not only associated with this diagnosis) in which consciousness becomes disconnected from memory, emotion, bodily senses, or other psychological functions, as a consequence of trauma. As a psychological defence, in the short term, it serves to protect children and adults from the horror that others inflict on them. In the longer term, it can prevent healing and recovery, in some cases even including loss of memory of the traumatic events themselves.

DID is a controversial diagnosis, but there is a large literature testifying to its association with a history of childhood abuse in a Christian context. Some argue that it is particularly associated with ritual abuse. The fluctuating appearance of different personalities, or alter egos ('alters'), is often identified within some Christian contexts as evidence of demon possession, but exorcism seems to make the condition worse, with published scientific evidence of adverse psychological and spiritual outcomes. Perhaps the most important thing to do for someone struggling with DID is *not* to subject them to deliverance ministry.

Eating disorders include anorexia nervosa and bulimia nervosa, as well as a number of other conditions. In anorexia nervosa there is a disorder of body image and fear of gaining weight, so that food intake is restricted and weight is lost. Untreated, anorexia nervosa can lead to death. In bulimia nervosa, binge eating is accompanied by efforts to prevent weight gain (e.g. self-induced vomiting), with the result that body mass index is usually kept within the normal range.

There has been much discussion as to whether or not the 'fasting saints' of early and medieval Christianity might have been suffering from anorexia nervosa. Angela of Foligno (1248–1309), for example, was said to have eaten nothing apart from the communion host for many years. While it is difficult to know what to make of these stories, and they are impossible to verify scientifically, it is clear that excessive fasting can easily get confusingly entangled with Christian spirituality. Bodily appetites and spiritual virtue are easily viewed as being in conflict, and extreme asceticism (including fasting) is sometimes justified as spiritually meritorious. In contrast to this view, Christian spirituality may not be so much about subduing the body, as being a good steward of it.

Addictions include not only addictions to drugs, including socially used drugs such as alcohol and nicotine, but also behaviours such as gambling. (Some would include a range of other addictive behaviours too, such as those involving sex, physical exercise or internet gaming.) In addiction, drug use (or other addictive behaviour) is persisted in despite the harm that it causes, both to the affected individual and to others, and is perceived as being difficult to control. While initially there might be denial that there is any problem, people struggling with addiction reach a point where they acknowledge that they want to stop the cycle of harmful behaviour, but find they can't.

In his letter to the Romans, St Paul talks about an inner conflict in which he says, 'I do not do what I want, but I do the very thing I hate' (7.15). Paul acknowledges both that there is a division within himself, due to sin, and that he wants to do what is good – even though he finds that this is a struggle. The answer, Paul says, is to be found in Jesus, who rescues him from this slavery to sin. A superficial reading can make it sound quite simple, and perhaps in some ways it is, but this is not a case of 'Become a Christian and life will all be easy!' Simplicity and easiness should not be confused. The first of the 12 steps of Alcoholics Anonymous is concerned with a person's admission of powerlessness over alcohol, but there are 11 more steps concerned with turning one's life over to God. Similarly, Paul has much more to say about life in Christ that goes beyond this initial step.

The category of **personality disorders** is one of the most controversial in ICD and DSM. Personality disorders, now sometimes referred to as 'complex emotional needs', are concerned with enduring and distressing patterns of relationships, behaviour and inner experience which begin in adolescence. Such conditions are often viewed by psychiatrists (although – it must be said – not all psychiatrists) as extremely difficult or impossible to treat. It might well be argued that this is simply a labelling of people who are different, that it is a way of giving up on people and that it is unhelpfully prejudicial and stigmatizing. However, the category includes a diverse group of conditions which are manifested in traits ranging from instability of emotions and relationships, through to paranoid suspiciousness, and antisocial disregard for others. Such problems are a cause of significant suffering and distress, both for the individual concerned and/or for those around them.

In the Gospels, Jesus shows concern for those who are marginalized, seen by others as 'unclean' or sinful, and who in various ways find themselves with an uncomfortable personal or social identity. It is hard to imagine that Jesus would not be concerned for people who might today be given the unhelpful label of 'personality disorder'. Moreover, we all struggle to some extent with relationships, with complex inner emotional needs or with being perceived by others as different. The issue here is partly one of the degree of distress and partly one of the perception of others. The spiritual challenges are for all of us. How do we respond to those who are different, or those whose emotional needs we perceive as being too difficult? Are we compassionate, inclusive and empathetic, or judgmental, exclusive and unsympathetic?

Neurocognitive disorders include a group of conditions for which underlying brain pathology is identifiable using diagnostic or post-mortem tests. Among other conditions in this group is a set of diseases known as the dementias. In dementia the disease process causes a progressive loss of cognitive functions, such as attention, orientation, memory, language skills and problem solving. There are often also disturbances of mood (e.g. irritability, sadness, withdrawal), and there may be delusions or hallucinations. These problems are often made worse due to the negative way in which others respond. The two most common forms of dementia are Alzheimer's disease and 'multi-infarct', or vascular, dementia. In most parts of the world, somewhere between 5 and 7 per cent of people over 60 are found to be suffering from dementia.

The dementias present a further spiritual challenge to us all. How caring are we towards those who are most vulnerable in our society? They also confront us with questions about what it means to be a person, or a Christian, as the faculties that enable us to know and be who we are in the world are gradually eroded and lost. For many people, their sense of self is concerned with a narrative history, a life story. Who am I when I can no longer remember my own story?

Prayer and mental health

It was suggested above that Christian spirituality is about prayer, and that prayer is about giving our attention to things in such a way that they become opportunities for us to participate in the life, death and resurrection of Jesus. How does mental illness have an impact on this life of prayer?

The giving of any kind of attention requires a range of cognitive faculties, including both memory and an ability to focus (or be selective). This selectivity operates both internally – in terms of things that we hold in our minds – and externally – in terms of our perceptions of the world around us. In prayer we make decisions (consciously or unconsciously) about the things that matter, and we hold them in our minds, offering them to God. We may then have many expectations about what happens next. Prayer is not magic; it is not about God doing what I command by means of a special ritual or formula. It is much more about how we open ourselves – our hearts and minds – to God.

What happens, then, when I am anxious or depressed, traumatized, struggling with cravings for food or drugs, preoccupied with a broken relationship, or unable to hold my attention or remember what it is that I want to pray for? In various ways, my ability to give my attention to things in prayer will be impaired. We might say that it will be a struggle to pray. However, at the same time, the things that are causing me to struggle to pray may become the focus of my prayers. As I struggle with these things, God is with me, in Christ. Whether or not I am aware of this presence (and in some cases, I may be feeling very painfully unaware!), my struggle – offered to God – becomes my prayer. Let us take just a couple of brief examples.

A young woman – let us call her Christine – is depressed. Christine is feeling negative and hopeless. She is not sure that she believes in God any more, but, if she does, she is sure that he is not pleased with her. She feels guilty for all kinds of things, some of which she would normally recognize as very minor things, and others of which are complete misapprehensions. Christine is lacking in energy to do things, she has lost her appetite, and she has thoughts of ending her life. Prayer has become impossible for Christine, in the sense that she normally understands it. She can't focus her thoughts, and in any case she feels distant from God. For Christine, this is now the place of her prayers. It is a dark place. Perhaps, in some ways, it is even a kind of 'dark night of the soul', as written about by John of the Cross (see Chapter 3), although I am not suggesting here that depression and the dark night are necessarily the same thing. (Someone might be depressed and not experiencing a dark night, or amid a dark night and not be depressed.) For Christine, prayer is now a real struggle, but it is a struggle *with* God, both in the sense that God is *with* her – perhaps most especially when she is not feeling his presence at all – and in the sense that she is struggling *with* God in that it might feel as though he has turned against her. In this dark place, Christine needs to know that others are praying for her, but she does not need unrealistic expectations placed on her to pray in ways that she cannot. The reality of her prayer is not measured by the extent to which she can remember things that she needs to pray for, the awareness that she has of God's presence, or her expectation that things might get better. It is beyond scientific measurement. It is something that God sees, but which Christine struggles to hold on to.

A 45-year-old man, whom we shall call Donald, is a member of a Charismatic church in which people are encouraged to see prayer as conversational, a two-way process in which God 'talks back' (to borrow a phrase used by American anthropologist Tanya Luhrmann in the title of her book, *When God Talks Back*). Donald regularly hears a voice in answer to his prayers, a voice which he believes is the voice of the Holy Spirit. The voice comforts, encourages and guides him in his daily life. All is well, until Donald loses his job, and initially becomes depressed. However, he soon experiences an elation of mood and hears the voice – which he still believes to be God – telling him to sell his house and possessions and preach the gospel on the streets of his home town. His doctor refers him to a psychiatrist who tells him that the voice he hears is just a part of an illness and he shouldn't listen to it. The psychiatrist prescribes medication, which initially makes Donald feel worse, and eventually he is admitted to hospital. Donald makes a good recovery, and when he is better he comes to distinguish between the voice that he heard when he was ill and the voice that he normally hears in prayer. He also sees his experience of illness (which he now recognizes definitely was an illness) as having brought him closer to God. However, his psychiatrist tells him that his faith is a part of the problem and that he should leave the church he attends. His friends in church treat him differently after his illness, and his experiences are dismissed as being a part of his illness rather than a part of his relationship with God. Donald struggles, not so much with God (although he does wonder why all of this has happened to him) as with mental health professionals and Christian friends, none of whom seem able to affirm what he believes has been a genuine encounter with God amid his illness.

For both Christine and Donald prayer has not been easy, but they have persevered. They have been differently encouraged, or discouraged, by those around them. Their mental health problems have become a part of their prayers, and have shaped their prayers, but their encounter with God amid these problems has not been any less valid because they have been given a diagnosis. Indeed, their encounters with God – difficult though they may have been – have probably been much more heartfelt and significant than those of many people not struggling with such problems. Spirituality may actually grow in such a context, rather than being stifled by it. Of course, that is not to say that it is always this way. For some, a mental health crisis may be a point of turning away from faith. For another person, not struggling with mental health issues, faith may grow and flourish differently. However, mental health and mental illness are all a part of the warp and weft of life within which prayer gets woven.

Conclusion

The message of this chapter, and this book, is therefore not that prayer amid mental health challenges is easy. It is not. Nor is it a platitude: 'Things may feel bad, but God will get you through.' (This may well be true, of course, but said in the wrong way it can be really unhelpful.) Rather, the message is that the things that we struggle with – the things that seem to stand in the way of our relationship with God – can actually be the context for our encounter with God. God is with us – in Christ – in the midst of our moments of weakness, and at the very times when we may feel far away from God. As St Paul wrote to the Corinthians, God's power is made perfect in weakness (2 Corinthians 12.9).

Biblical reflection

Jacob was left alone; and a man wrestled with him until daybreak. When the man saw that he did not prevail against Jacob, he struck him on the hip socket; and Jacob's hip was put out of joint as he wrestled with him. Then he said, 'Let me go, for the day is breaking.' But Jacob said, 'I will not let you go, unless you bless me.' So he said to him, 'What is your name?' And he said, 'Jacob.' Then the man said, 'You shall no longer be called Jacob, but Israel, for you have striven with God and with humans, and have prevailed.'
(Genesis 32.24–28)

Jacob has had a chequered life so far. He may be one of the great ancestors of Israel, but he has not found faith, relationships and life particularly easy. Jacob struggles: he struggles with family, with people more generally, and he struggles with God. There are no obvious reasons why he should. He just, simply, struggles, and seems to feel that everyone in life is likely to be against him. He behaves as if everything good in life has to be fought for, hard won. Years before, Jacob had met God in the desert. He had been running away from his brother, in fear for his life, after tricking his father into giving him his brother's blessing – as if blessings were rationed. In the desert, God spontaneously offered a promise to Jacob, but Jacob tried to negotiate for what was freely offered (Genesis 32–33). He is not sure about God, not sure that life can ever treat him well.

Here, years later, he meets a stranger in the same desert. God is no longer immediately recognizable; God is the stranger who meets Jacob in the night, in the darkness. God does not simply offer a blessing, but wrestles with Jacob silently. God meets Jacob where Jacob is, on his terms, engaging in a way that Jacob can understand. The God of all creation chooses to make himself an equal wrestling partner with struggling Jacob. Surely God could have overcome instantly. God could have prevailed by force. God could have argued, or tried to prove to Jacob that his understanding or approach was flawed. But God does not do that. God wrestles in the dark, all night.

Jacob does relate to God – but his way of relating is not the open faith of Abraham or the risk-taking faith of Moses. It struggles and fights and asks questions. There is no condemnation of Jacob, no judgement or comparison about his faith. God will come to be known as 'the God of Abraham, Isaac and Jacob'. Jacob is no less a person than anyone else for struggling with God: like others before and many after, he is, ultimately, blessed by God.

The blessing does not erase the struggle, nor does it change everything. Jacob will bear the signs of the struggle as he goes on, through a persistent limp. Yet the signs of his struggle become an embodied sign of hope for all those who come after: he is to become known as 'Israel', a name that speaks of struggle (in Hebrew, Israel means 'wrestles with God'). The faith of Israel is not an easy faith; it is one born out of persistent struggle with God, and it is out of this struggle that both pain and blessing arise to form a story that has shaped the world for centuries, and still speaks today of hope in the midst of struggles in the darkness.

We may want to ask ourselves, in our Christian communities, how significant it is that so much of the story of Scripture centres on a people whose name, Israel, is about struggle and wrestling. How can this help us speak well of what it means to live a life of faith? How might it help us care for one another when we struggle?

Prayers

A prayer for those who struggle
Loving God,
we pray for all those who struggle
with life, with faith, with wellbeing.
We ask that you would meet them within the struggle
and comfort and strengthen them.
Amen

A prayer in the midst of struggle

O God of Jacob,
I also feel that I am struggling in the night,
struggling to know who you are,
struggling to know where you are,
and whether you intend good things.
Like Jacob, I want blessing
yet I do not know what blessing looks like,
or how hard it will be to live with.
Meet me in the struggle
so that I may see your face.
Amen

Questions to facilitate individual/group study

1 How did you think about mental wellbeing before reading this chapter? Has anything you have read challenged you, or helped you, or pushed you to develop your thinking in any way?

2 Is there anything you would like to explore in more detail?

3 What do you worry about? What have you been told about worrying in the churches you have attended and books you have read?

4 What would the 'good life', or 'abundant life', look like for you? How might this help, or hinder, how you approach mental health challenges?

5 Has anyone you know experienced a major mental illness? How would that person describe the challenges he or she has faced? How did this interact with his or her faith and spirituality?

6 Are there parts of Scripture that seem particularly relevant to you in relation to mental wellbeing and mental health challenges? Are they helpful? Are some of them negative? Why is that?

7 How often do people in your church or faith community speak about mental health challenges? What kind of language do they use? In what setting does this happen? Could this be done more, or in better ways?

8 Is it mental health we struggle with, or is it mental ill health?

Pointers to further reading

Cook, C. C. H. (2018), 'Alcohol and Other Addictions', in B. Geary and J. Bryan (eds), *Pastoral Challenges and Concerns: A Christian handbook for leaders*, Stowmarket, Kevin Mayhew, pp. 91–118.

—— (2020), *Christians Hearing Voices: Affirming experience and finding meaning*, London, Jessica Kingsley.

—— (2020), 'What Did Jesus Have to Say about Mental Health?', in C. C. H. Cook and I. Hamley (eds), *The Bible and Mental Health: Towards a biblical theology of mental health*, London, SCM Press, pp. 128–40.

—— (2021), 'Worry and Prayer: Some Reflections on the Psychology and Spirituality of Jesus's Teaching on Worry', in R. Manning (ed.), *Mutual Enrichment between Psychology and Theology*, London, Routledge, pp. 163–75.

Cook, C. C. H., and I. Hamley (eds) (2020), *The Bible and Mental Health: Towards a biblical theology of mental health*, London, SCM Press.

Hastings, S. (2020), *Wrestling with My Thoughts: A doctor with mental illness discovers strength*, London, IVP.

Luhrmann, T. M. (2012), *When God Talks Back: Understanding the American Evangelical relationship with God*, New York, NY, Knopf.

Swinton, J. (2012), *Dementia: Living in the memories of God*, Grand Rapids, MI, Eerdmans.

—— (2020), *Finding Jesus in the Storm: The spiritual lives of Christians with mental health challenges*, Grand Rapids, MI, Eerdmans.

Chapter references

American Psychiatric Association (2013), *Diagnostic and Statistical Manual of Mental Disorders, Fifth Edition* (DSM-5), Washington, DC, American Psychiatric Association.

Weil, S. (1952), *Gravity and Grace*, London, Routledge & Kegan Paul.

2

Stigma and prejudice: giving up negative attitudes

As he walked along, he saw a man blind from birth. His disciples asked him, 'Rabbi, who sinned, this man or his parents, that he was born blind?' Jesus answered, 'Neither this man nor his parents sinned; he was born blind so that God's works might be revealed in him. We must work the works of him who sent me while it is day; night is coming when no one can work. As long as I am in the world, I am the light of the world.' When he had said this, he spat on the ground and made mud with the saliva and spread the mud on the man's eyes, saying to him, 'Go, wash in the pool of Siloam' (which means Sent). Then he went and washed and came back able to see. The neighbours and those who had seen him before as a beggar began to ask, 'Is this not the man who used to sit and beg?' Some were saying, 'It is he.' Others were saying, 'No, but it is someone like him.' He kept saying, 'I am the man.' But they kept asking him, 'Then how were your eyes opened?' He answered, 'The man called Jesus made mud, spread it on my eyes, and said to me, "Go to Siloam and wash." Then I went and washed and received my sight.' They said to him, 'Where is he?' He said, 'I do not know.'

They brought to the Pharisees the man who had formerly been blind. Now it was a sabbath day when Jesus made the mud and opened his eyes. Then the Pharisees also began to ask him how he had received his sight. He said to them, 'He put mud on my eyes. Then I washed, and now I see.' Some of the Pharisees said, 'This man is not from God, for he does not observe the sabbath.' But others said, 'How can a man who is a sinner perform such signs?' And they were divided. So they said again to the blind man, 'What do you say about him? It was your eyes he opened.' He said, 'He is a prophet.' (John 9.1–17)

This story of Jesus healing a man who was born blind is well known. It is one of many encounters in the Gospel of John, encounters that challenge and reshape the faith and expectations of those who meet Jesus, and of the disciples and the ever-present crowds. The man was born blind and, as we see in the story, had been reduced to sitting on the side of the road, begging. Why should this be? As the account continues, it becomes clear that he has parents, who care enough to come when summoned. He is known in the community; people know who he is and who his family is. Why should he sit in loneliness and destitution? People probably passed him regularly, knowing he was there. But for now, something interrupts the flow of a normal day: Jesus *sees* him. He is no longer invisible, someone to ignore or avoid. He is seen, and being seen prompts the disciples' uncomfortable question, 'Who sinned, this man or his parents?' The disciples' first reaction is not one of compassion, let alone pity. Their first reaction is one that ignores the real person in front of them, and turns him into a problem to be solved, a puzzle to be answered. The disciples do not see the man. The disciples do not speak to him; they speak *about* him. Just like his neighbours who, a little later on, will first speak about him, then ask one another questions, all while the man keeps talking, unacknowledged and disbelieved.

In contrast, Jesus speaks to the man, and gives him a choice: he can go to the pool of Siloam and wash, or he could refuse. He is seen; he is a person, with agency and choices. Jesus does not assume that he cannot look after himself or cannot do anything, but assumes that he has far more ability and independence than he is granted by his neighbours, who have reduced him to a 'beggar'. The disciples' question highlights the beliefs and imagination of their culture around illness and disability. They assume a link between disability and sin; they project moral categories onto simple physical facts. Maybe they look for explanations of a phenomenon they find frightening. After all, if you believe that misfortunes are due to sin, then it must be possible to avoid them. Disciples and neighbours seem unable to see the man; all they see is his blindness. He is reduced to part of himself, and then even this part is interpreted in ways that make assumptions about the whole of who he is: tainted, different, other, not able to participate in their version of life.

When something changes and the man is healed, they cannot reconcile this 'new' person with the one they knew, because it challenges their belief. Surely if the man's blindness was due to sin, then he wouldn't be healed by a rabbi? Their beliefs not only prevent them from seeing the man at the beginning of the story, but also prevent them from seeing the man he is becoming. Jesus, in contrast, sees the man from the start, and challenges others to start seeing him too. He tells the disciples that their reading of the situation is wrong (there is no connection with sin), and instead connects the man with the glory of God. Implicitly, he tells them that their un-seeing, their condemnation, is preventing them from seeing God at work, and that God can work in and through every person – not just the people they may consider worthy of the attention or gaze of God. Every person is seen by God.

The story refers to a physical disability, but it is typical of the way in which stigma works and attaches itself to various conditions. When we come to mental health, many who struggle with mental health challenges report similar experiences to the ones in this passage: they may be told that they are not spiritual enough, or praying enough, or trying hard enough, not believing the right things, not having enough faith – all of which are simply different versions of the disciples' question, 'Who sinned?' In the same way, they may quickly find that rather than answering the question 'How are you?' truthfully, it is easier to hide, to pretend, so that they are not fully seen, because their neighbours prefer to walk on by and ignore what they are going through. In all too many churches there is a similar attitude; church leaders and members rarely think of cherishing those who struggle with mental health challenges as people in whom the glory of God can be seen. Fortunately, if there is anything we know about Jesus, it is that these kinds of barriers do not hold for him. In every story, he attends to the full humanity of those he meets, and challenges others to do so too.

Understanding stigma

It is helpful at this point to think a little more about 'stigma'. Why is it such a widespread phenomenon? How does it work, and what is its impact?

Stigma is based on the assumptions we all make about people, and the way in which human beings tend to sort the world into categories. This is not a negative tendency in itself; categorizing, making generalizations, enables us to understand the world around us and not have to start with first principles in every encounter. So, for instance, think of encounters with animals: there are enough animals on four legs who miaow and have other features in common with one another that we can recognize them as 'cats'. We form a category. There can be many different cats in that category, hugely different from one another. But having a 'cat' category means that we have some idea of what to do, or not to do, when we meet a new four-legged miaower. We know they might scratch us; we know they may be shy; we know they may like being stroked and will show their appreciation through purring; we know that pulling their tail is unlikely to be a good idea. The general category guides our behaviour, but it does not tell us what kind of cat this is, whether it is a friendly cat, a scaredy cat, a playful cat, a lazy cat, a bird-catcher or a mouser, and so on. Nor does it tell us whether it is a 'typical' cat. Some cats are very placid and unlikely to scratch. The general rule always needs to be tested against the particular cat you may happen to meet.

Categories enable us to understand the world and make sense of it, seeing patterns, connections and shapes, and these then shape how we respond, react and interact. Our thinking in categories is a trait of animal instinct and survival, which helps us assess new situations, people or questions faster. Problems arise, however, if our categorizing proves to be incorrect but we refuse to change it, or if our categorizing becomes overlaid with negative, caricatural expectations that do not reflect the truth, and lead us to behave in negative ways. To go back to the cat example, if I develop a prejudice that all cats scratch and therefore all cats are dangerous, it may lead me to treat cats badly, to prevent them from getting cared for, and it will certainly prevent me from getting to know any one cat and discovering the amazing gift of friendship with this animal. If others agree with me, and together we influence wider culture, then all cats will suffer from the reputation they have, however unfounded, and individual prejudice will lead to widespread stigma.

Our problem, as human beings, is that we do not apply this categorizing just to things and animals; we also apply it to people. And to form these categories, we draw largely on culture and commonly held views, which guide and shape our experience. The normal ways in which we categorize people become warped, and we attach value judgements to certain traits and characteristics. When a certain group of people is consistently characterized negatively, then 'stigma' develops. The people in this group may be very different from one another, but they stop being 'seen' in their difference. They are reduced to the one thing they may have in common and are judged by their belonging to this category. Their identity is reduced, taken away, and they are neither seen nor met as full human beings. This is what happens in our story of Jesus and the blind man: the man was ignored, people talked about him, and he was not allowed to be a full part of the community he inhabited.

The word 'stigma' comes from the ancient Greek language and culture. It referred to a bodily sign designed to expose or mark out something. It could be the branding of a slave, who then was seen as less than a full human being, reduced to property; it could be a sign cut or burnt into the body of a criminal or traitor, in which case the person would bear shame in his or her body, and every new interaction would be tainted by suspicion and distrust. Over time, the word widened beyond the physical mark itself, and now it refers primarily to the negative perception of someone's status, or a part of who that person is. Stigma is intimately connected to one's identity and relationships. It is a feature of one's identity that becomes stigmatized, discounted or 'spoiled', to use sociologist Irvine Goffman's word (Goffman, 1990), and it overshadows all other aspects of identity.

Goffman is helpful in pointing out that stigma is primarily a *relational* concept. It is about the expectations that one individual has of another, the things he or she may unconsciously consider 'normal' or 'desirable', and about the shaping of both individuals' perception of their identity, and how they may be able to relate to each other. It is precisely the unspoken idea of what the ideal or norm might be that is so damaging to identity. On the one hand, if I am the person who bears the stigma, I am seen as falling short of some ideal humanity; I am seen as somewhat less than human, and others may relate to me condescendingly, or fearfully, or try to avoid me. On the other hand, if you are the person who sees yourself as somehow more 'ideal', stigma bears with it the fear of losing control of your world, of losing your identity, and therefore makes it harder should you, one day, come to share in the lived reality of those who are stigmatized. Neither person in the relationship can be fully human any more, because the reality of human vulnerability, of difference, is seen as negative, as something to avoid, rather than something to inhabit and understand together. In addition, when those who suffer are faced with stigma and negative beliefs in others, they can easily come to believe these things about themselves, and internalize the stigma, which in turn will exacerbate their struggles. Stigma therefore can be both a response to, and a cause of, mental health problems.

Stigma at work

The story of Job, in the Old Testament, illustrates this dynamic perfectly. Job was a man who had everything; in many ways, he was the 'ideal' man of the time, the kind of person others aspired to be – rich, with a lovely family, pious and good. He ticked every box of the 'good guy' ideal. However, disaster strikes, and he loses everything – his family, his wealth, his health. Job is deeply traumatized and initially in such shock that he sits in silence for an entire week. His reaction is entirely understandable and appropriate to the level of disaster he has experienced. His entire world has collapsed, and nothing makes sense. Shock and silence are followed by anger and bitterness, and the endless, unanswered question, 'Why?'

Job has friends; they come to surround him when they hear the news. However, Job's friends are not comfortable with this 'new' Job. Job is no longer the confident spiritual leader he has been; instead, he shouts at God and demands answers. Faith is no longer a comfort, and God has become a problem for Job, and his friends struggle with that. His friends are used to the belief that if all goes well in life, it is because you deserve it, and God has blessed you. But if this has happened to Job, then either their beliefs about life are wrong, or it is Job who has done something wrong to deserve this. Job's friends find it easier to blame Job than to accept that the world is less predictable, less safe, than they would like it to be. And so we have many chapters of arguments between Job and his friends. His friends try to fit Job into the category of 'sinner', both because of his misfortunes and because of the way in which trauma has led him to question his previous certainties. For Job, this is devastating. Not only has he lost everything, not only is he deeply traumatized, but the very people he was counting on to be on his side now see his distress as a moral taint, a sign of failure, and they refuse to walk with him towards a new way of understanding the world and relating to God.

The wider world that is portrayed as Job's world was one that stigmatized poverty, illness and mental anguish. They were seen as signs of moral deficiency. To challenge this belief would have been to challenge the friends' certainties about the world, their sense of identity, and the idea that being rich, or comfortable and healthy, was their right, rooted in their own efforts, and instead portray these as an undeserved blessing. They would have had to face their own fragility and vulnerability, and it was somehow too difficult or frightening for them to do that. In their refusal, they belittle Job and diminish his experience; but they also bar themselves from being able to see the world as it is and relate to a God who is much bigger than their expectations. At the end of the book of Job, it is Job who meets God and who hears God's words of approval. God tells Job, 'You have spoken what is right' whereas he condemns the friends' speech (Job 42.7). Job's identity may have been spoiled in his friends' eyes, but before God, Job stood whole. In this story, his struggles with God were seen by his friends as a cause for stigma. In contrast, what the story as a whole tells us is that Job's honesty and struggles were not outside the bounds of God's presence, but were a valid and essential expression of faith in the midst of utter darkness.

We can read this story and think that Job's friends were a little harsh, or that we would not be quite so mistaken today. However, the stories of people with mental health challenges tell us otherwise.

Meet, for instance, Amelia. Amelia grew up in a middle-class family that appeared to be a good, ideal family from the outside. However, behind closed doors, her father was violent and emotionally abusive, consistently telling her she was ugly, fat and lazy. As a teenager, Amelia developed bulimia. She would eat large amounts and make herself sick so she would not put on weight. For a long time she kept this secret, as she felt no one would understand and people would judge her. She tried to stop herself overeating, but the more she tried, the worse it got. After several years of struggling, she had forgotten what it was like to eat normally and avoided eating in front of anyone else. One day, she felt so desperate, so out of control, that she sat with a box of pills for several hours and considered ending her own life. At that point, she felt she had to try to speak to someone. She went to a teacher she trusted and told her what was going on. The teacher's first response was, 'You're far too clever for this.' She had an image in her head of the person that Amelia was – educated, middle-class, privileged in some ways – and when the reality of mental health challenges broke through, she could not cope with the discrepancy. The teacher's underlying belief seems to have been that mental health is somehow more under our control than physical health; or that somehow mental health and intelligence are related.

Amelia had already been aware of negative portrayals of bulimia; the stigma was reinforced tenfold, even a hundredfold, by this encounter, with the result that she was driven to hide to an even greater degree, and it was several years before she sought help again. Her story illustrates the power of stigma – it often drives sufferers to hide, to shield part of their identity out of shame; revealing this part of their identity is risky. If they let others see the whole of who they are, then the risk of rejection is high, and, as Amelia experienced, the reaction of others can reinforce all the negative thoughts they already felt. Stigma is not just a *result* of mental health challenges; it also reinforces the challenges.

In both of these stories, stigma leads to negative reactions of rejection. But this is not always the case. Stigma can also lead us to want to act benevolently, kindly, to treat the other person as if he or she is in need of our help, of our fixing. Or it can lead to a kind of awkwardness, a fear of saying the wrong thing, which paralyses interaction. Either way, however, stigmatized people are not being treated as fully human. They are consistently made to feel different. Their identity is somehow diminished, and mental ill health can become the defining factor in their relationships, so that the whole person is no longer seen. In the case of Amelia, her teacher could not see how she could be *both* a clever person *and* someone struggling with bulimia; she felt she had to see either one or the other. She could not see the whole of Amelia.

Stigma and expectations

There is a close relationship between stigma and what we expect – from ourselves and from others – and, perhaps, what we desire. When another person shows us a part of reality that contradicts our expectations, or a part of reality we would rather avoid, it is easy to react in a way similar to Job's friends; or, when we experience mental health challenges for ourselves, to try to hide, or behave in ways that will seem like our 'normal self' to those who know us.

Where do these expectations come from? And how can we become aware of them, and challenge them when appropriate? Some of our expectations reflect an ideal of an independent, self-sufficient adult, who works, plays, has relationships, cares for his or her appearance, and so on. Of course, no one does all of these things perfectly, or without some struggles. But outwardly, we rarely share deep inner struggles, particularly in the world of contemporary social media selfies and status updates. If we meet a 'real' person, and this person acknowledges, or simply cannot hide, his or her struggles, this is often seen as not being as competent an adult as one should be. It is helpful, though, to wonder whether our ideas of independence, of 'coping', actually rely on ideals of heroism and on flawed concepts of what it is to be a person. Human beings are never fully independent: at the most basic level, for survival, we need to work together as a species. We cannot grow into functioning adults without a vast array of others enabling us to do so; as adults, we still depend on complex economic and social systems. But these systems easily hide our dependence on one another. Instead of farming together, or hunting together, as in times past or in other societies, we might work at a job and then use the money this generates to buy what others have produced. Or we might be retired, or out of work, or in receipt of benefits, all of which draw on a complex economic network of solidarity. We are still depending on one another, but the actual persons we depend on are less visible, less connected to us.

When I (Isabelle) was a university chaplain, I met a young woman from the Middle East who had come to the UK with her husband, who was doing a PhD. Without a visa of her own, she was not entitled to work. Her English was too poor for her to study. Stuck at home with few acquaintances, she started to sink into a deep depression. In one of our conversations, she told me: 'I feel so alone here. No one understands me. Back home, I had six sisters. I was never alone in my whole life until I came to the UK. We were always together. Always talking, always laughing, always singing. It wasn't always easy, but no one leaves you on your own like this in my home country.'

When the young woman tried to express her feelings to others around her in the UK, they told her to make the most of it, to sort herself out, to make more of an effort, that she should enjoy having space. Unsurprisingly, it did not help. Besides feeling depressed, she started feeling judged and ashamed, as if she was not competent, with others telling her that she was being needy, like a child. But listening to her, I could not help but wonder: what if the problem is the other way round? What if the problem really is with the assumption that human beings are independent, can flourish on their own, and have to be the masters of their own destiny? This student's dad eventually came to stay with her, and he simply could not understand a society where people would leave a woman alone all day, in a group of flats with other people, all equally alone, for so many hours. He understood her: her struggles were struggles that made sense, that he *expected*, given the conditions of her life. She was the same person, with the same mental health challenges, but in the UK they were a source of stigma, whereas in her home country they gave rise to a community rallying around her. Her own family, in turn, started caricaturing people in the UK as uncaring. Underlying the different reactions was a different concept of identity and personhood, and how 'normal' people may feel and react to their circumstances. While there were challenges specific to this woman's culture too, her culture's focus on community relationships enabled her to expect to reach out for help and to think of receiving help as normal and appropriate, rather than as a sign that she was somehow deficient. She was used to bearing burdens with others rather than on her own. The expectation of independence and 'dealing with stuff' heightens stigma for those who struggle.

Another feature of Western societies makes them potentially prone to stigmatizing those with mental health challenges. As a society that cherishes science, proof and rationality, the experiences of people with mental health challenges, and in particular mental illness, can seem strange, inexplicable, and therefore both more threatening and easier to ignore or dismiss. The search for physical and medical explanations can be elusive, and in the absence of either a definable 'cause' or a remedy, people with mental health challenges are sometimes dismissed as not really ill, or, alternatively, as simply beyond help. Either of these attitudes is corrosive. On the one hand, for those struggling with severe depression, being told to 'pull yourself together' simply adds to the burdens they are carrying, by implying they are not really trying, or that there *is* a solution but for some reason they choose not to embrace it. On the other hand, people struggling with a severe mental illness can often be made to feel that they have been given a terminal diagnosis, that they can never get better, or live a good life, even though mental illness can fluctuate and manifest in hugely different ways in different people (Swinton, 2020). The Western tendency to focus on 'intellect, reason and clarity of thinking' can be destructive for those who see and engage with the world differently because of mental health challenges. 'In such a cultural milieu, mental health challenges can easily be perceived as challenging each of these socially valued attributes and, in so doing, challenging our conceptions of what it means to be fully human' (Swinton, 2020, p. 16).

Here it is helpful to turn to some of the Bible's descriptions of what it means to be 'fully human'. While the idea of 'body, mind, and soul' is a popular one, it is not consistent with the Christian Scriptures, implying as it does three separate parts of a person, with a hierarchy of importance between these. The human person in the Old Testament in particular is a whole person, not a separate intellectual or spiritual centre housed in a bodily envelope. A person is someone in relation with others, with human beings, with God, with the natural world. A human being is, first and foremost, a creature of God – loved, cared for, created in God's image. The word 'identity' does not appear in Scripture, nor does the concept of identity as we know it. Yet, in trying to find an approximation, what we see is that identity is derived first and foremost from being made in God's image; it is this image that defines worth – regardless of the differences that mark out human beings, in their bodies, in their minds, in their ways of being. Intelligence is nowhere seen as a marker of additional moral worth. Neither is independence, or rationality, or health, or happiness. If we come back to Job, we see that he had lost everything and struggled to even articulate faith in a way that was recognizable to others. Indeed, rational thought seemed to get in the way, and Job does not seem too sure about God at all. But none of this diminishes Job as a human being loved by God – as the end of the story shows. Job is not defined by his struggles or reduced to them. Neither is his faith defined by them.

When God is part of the problem

The story of Job draws our attention to a specific aspect of stigma: what happens when God and the community of faith are part of the problem. Christians have expectations of what 'faith' and 'being a Christian' look like. These expectations might include how we talk about and to God, participation in religious activity, prayer and reading the Bible, the content of belief, and so on. Mental health challenges can disrupt these expectations, as in the story of Job. The disruption can lead to stigma and rejection of a spirituality that seems strange or challenging, or that even threatens to question received wisdom.

Yet, if we read the Scriptures, and if we look at the writings of people of faith over the centuries, we quickly see that faith comes in many different shapes and sizes, and that different ways of expressing faith (or struggling with faith) are part of the texture, breadth and richness of the human experience of life with God. The Psalms are a great treasury of human prayers, and they span the whole gamut of possible emotions. Some are positive, full of praise and faith. But many talk of struggle, of God's apparent absence; they express anger and pain in the shape of lament. While they often juxtapose these feelings of doubt, anger and challenging God with a remaining sense of hope, two psalms, 88 and 137, do not, and linger in an overwhelming sense of hopelessness. Because they are written *to* God, these 'lament psalms', despite their negative outlook, still remain part of what 'faith' looks like. They speak of those times when God is the problem, or when God seems irretrievably absent or disinterested. They speak of unanswered prayer. Faith does not take away what may seem to be despair, trauma or depression. Because these psalms are in Scripture, they demand that Christians should make space for these emotions and expressions within their life together. Yet in most Western churches, lament is noticeably absent from worship, liturgy and hymns, and this absence can easily lead us to stigmatize those who express life in this way, as if doing so were somehow at odds with faith, rather than, as Scripture shows, an essential part of the experience and reality of the people of God. We could look at other parts of Scripture and see people hearing voices, or having strange experiences or visions, all of which, in the context of twenty-first-century Western cultures, would seem odd and easily stigmatized, yet was accepted and recognized as a way to hear God in biblical times, and for much of history.

The Bible does not uncritically validate every human experience, or way of speaking of God, of course. But it makes space for real human beings, and the whole of human life, and brings out the possibility of discerning the work and glory of God – to return to the passage in John's Gospel – in the *whole* of life.

Stigma in churches is not simply about expectations regarding how we might pray, or not want to pray, or the content of what we might say about God. It is also, partly, about what we imagine 'fullness of life' to be – the Gospel of John talks about living life to the full, of Jesus giving 'abundant life'. What is abundant life? And how do our ideas of what 'abundant life' looks like shape our response to others – and ourselves – when things go wrong or are difficult? Another way of asking the question is this: is our idea of the life that Jesus gives us, or invites us into, spacious and generous enough to include the whole of human circum- stances? Abundant life with God clearly cannot be turned into a life of ease, comfort or happiness. Jesus encourages his disciples to take their cross and follow him. Jesus speaks of both fullness of life and bearing one's cross; these two things highlight the paradox of the life of faith: it can be abundant at the same time as challenging and full of pain. The life that disciples are invited into is a life of relationships – with God and with one another – a life where love is practised, but, first and foremost, a life which starts with God's love for us. It is a life based on every person being made in God's image, with one's identity safe and secure within God. As Paul says: 'your life is hidden with Christ in God' (Colossians 3.3).

Finally, unhelpful expectations in churches may also manifest themselves quite prosaically. I once had a student training to be a vicar who was on placement in a large, buzzing, active church. As I sat down with him to talk about his placement, he shared that he felt that despite all its 'shiny' worship and activities, the church was quite a difficult place, without very much space for people who struggled. He described how the main minister there had once said to him, 'The thing is, if you have good pastoral care, you just attract needy people; but if you do mission, you attract leaders.' 'Needy people', many of them with mental health challenges, were stigmatized and reduced to one aspect of their selves – their need. They were not seen as full persons. That church leader's expectation of what 'church' was was driven by anxiety to grow the church, to 'do', and an underlying fear of vulnerability. He was not able to see that within vulnerability, there were gifts to be shared with the whole church. In many ways, it is a vision dramatically at odds with the vision of the Church in the New Testament. The people whom Jesus gathers around him, and who follow him, don't tend to be strong, wealthy or independent. They tend to be people who struggle, people who have been healed from deep distress, such as Mary Magdalene; people who get things wrong, such as Peter; and people who needed to turn away from everything they considered their status or strength, such as the apostle Paul. The community of followers of Jesus was a community of the weak and needy: it was a community of the redeemed, of those who knew they needed God – and one another.

Examining these expectations of what 'church' and 'faith' look like, and how they are expressed, is a first step in dealing with stigma, with the things we tell ourselves about either ourselves or others, which become a barrier and a burden.

Confronting stigma: reaching in, reaching out

Stigma can feel like a giant octopus with many tentacles – there isn't just one unhelpful narrative or expectation to combat, but many of them, and even when we successfully deal with one arm, another one seems to appear from nowhere. There may be no silver bullet, but that isn't to say that nothing can be done. Recognizing stigma and unhelpful narratives, in ourselves and others, is a useful step. None of us are ever 'neutral', or endlessly positively open to others. All of us have stories we tell ourselves and others that are unhelpful, that damage us and other people, that caricature or reduce another person to less than a full human being. Maybe being honest about this tendency to judge is an essential step in dealing with stigma. This tendency is also what makes stigma difficult to fight, because it involves changing many people, all in the same direction, so that an entire culture or world view can be altered. Stigma is something we can only change *together*.

Let's consider the expectations we have looked at throughout this chapter:

- What do I/we think are the essential aspects of 'being human'?
- What do I/we think is 'normal', and how does this shape my/our perceptions of mental health challenges?
- What do I/we expect 'faith' to look like?
- What does 'abundant life' look like?
- What might I/we be afraid of when it comes to mental health challenges?
- What does my/our culture tell me/us about mental health challenges?
- How do I/we think Christians should approach mental health challenges?
- What kinds of emotions and expressions does my/our community of faith encourage in the context of worship and prayer?

Asking these questions (and many others!) can help us become more aware of what shapes, or misshapes, some of our attitudes and responses, and begin to explore how we may change some of these expectations and the behaviours that derive from them.

Scripture, once again, can be a friend in the process. The Psalms, already mentioned, give us a much broader vocabulary for talking to and of God, and the life of faith, than we usually employ. Looking at the life of Jesus also uncovers a pattern of consistent challenge of stigma, as we saw in the story of the man born blind. This story is not unique; in fact it is paradigmatic: it is a type of story repeated so often that it is a trademark of the ministry of Jesus. Jesus crosses barriers and confounds expectations.

One of the Church of England's prayers for Holy Communion proclaims: 'he touched untouchables with love'.[5]

The ministry of Jesus was characterized by his love for those who were marginalized or excluded, those not considered good enough because of gender, race, social status, occupation, health, or because of their own choices and actions. In other words, Jesus challenged stigma by crossing barriers, by attending to real people. Jesus saw people for the whole of who they were; he did not reduce them to just one part of their identity, or to something they had done, or to the way they appeared. Jesus had *rich* interactions. It is striking to follow the theme of 'seeing' in Scripture. There are many passages that refer to God 'seeing' and God responding, for example in the story of Hagar, Ishmael's mother, driven into the desert by mistreatment. God sees her and talks to her, and she in turn calls God El-Roi, the 'God who saw me'. In Egypt, where the Hebrew people struggle and groan under slavery, God *sees* their pain, and responds. In the Gospels, again and again, Jesus *sees* and responds. Challenging stigma means making space to see the other person, so that he or she is visible as a full human being, known and loved by God.

Sometimes, it is also making space for people to allow themselves to be seen too. In one story, in the Gospel of Mark, a woman approaches Jesus from behind, not wanting to be seen, and touches the fringes of his garment. She had been shunned, ill for so long, that not only did others not 'see' her, but she too made every effort not to be seen. She did not seem to see herself as worthy to be seen, or helped, by Jesus either. Jesus' response is extraordinary: he stops, and heals the woman; he stops, and enables everyone else to see this woman too. And before the crowd, he draws attention to the whole person: not just someone who had been ill a long time, who was desperate and in pain, but a person of great faith, someone through whom others could see God – if they just bothered to stop and look. In this story, Jesus proclaims that this woman is just as worthy to be seen, and healed, as the daughter of the leader of the synagogue, Jairus. Jesus equalizes the people he talks to, and thereby makes it possible for them to relate as full human beings.

---

5 *Common Worship*, Eucharistic Prayer D.

The ministry of Jesus tells anyone reading or hearing Scripture one thing: that he or she is welcome, and cherished, and valued, with no exception. It is an invitation to allow ourselves to be seen by God, or, if that is simply too frightening, at least to begin to see ourselves and other people through the filter of God's love. It is also an invitation to us to establish a different way of relating to one another, one that is based on making space for the real people we are. The people whom Jesus meets and relates to are not cardboard people; they are neither 'saints' nor irredeemable sinners, neither fully good nor fully bad. They are complex people, full of contradictions and doubts, and they are invited to love God and one another. Encountering these stories and allowing them to ask questions of us today – about how we see ourselves, how we see one another and how we see God – may be the beginning of addressing stigma among us.

Conclusion

Stigma is a spoiled identity based on negative assumptions that we make about groups of people. Mental illnesses, mental health challenges, are sadly associated with stigma in a way that physical health conditions, for the most part, are not. For Christians, God and church become a part of the problem when we make unjustified negative assumptions about what the faith, the conversation about God, or the Christian life of others should look like. In Scripture, Job was a victim of stigma of this kind. In the Gospels we find that Jesus consistently spoke out against stigma and crossed the barriers that stigma creates. In the Psalms we find a language for talking to God which expands the restricted vocabulary that we so often employ because of the negative assumptions that we make about what may and may not be said to God in prayer. As Christians, we are called to follow Jesus' example and to see people through the filter of God's love.

Biblical reflection

As he walked along, he saw a man blind from birth. His disciples asked him, 'Rabbi, who sinned, this man or his parents, that he was born blind?' Jesus answered, 'Neither this man nor his parents

sinned; he was born blind so that God's works might be revealed in him. We must work the works of him who sent me while it is day; night is coming when no one can work. As long as I am in the world, I am the light of the world.' When he had said this, he spat on the ground and made mud with the saliva and spread the mud on the man's eyes, saying to him, 'Go, wash in the pool of Siloam' (which means Sent). Then he went and washed and came back able to see. The neighbours and those who had seen him before as a beggar began to ask, 'Is this not the man who used to sit and beg?' Some were saying, 'It is he.' Others were saying, 'No, but it is someone like him.' He kept saying, 'I am the man.' But they kept asking him, 'Then how were your eyes opened?' He answered, 'The man called Jesus made mud, spread it on my eyes, and said to me, "Go to Siloam and wash." Then I went and washed and received my sight.' They said to him, 'Where is he?' He said, 'I do not know.'
(John 9.1–12)

Spend a little time reading this passage over and over. What might the man born blind be feeling? I wonder how he thought about himself and his life. What were his hopes? Did he even have any?

What can it mean to be shunned and reduced to part of who you are, so that people no longer 'see' you, and talk *about* you but not *with* you?

The man is simply there as life goes on around him. Others seem neither to care nor to consider him fully human. They certainly do not think he has the potential to contribute to their life together, or to their understanding of God. His identity is ignored, damaged, spoiled by those around him. What might his prayer have been like? Full of pain, supplication, rage? Or mere resignation?

His life and plight are not unique; but in the universe of the Gospel, his life and plight are not inevitabilities. There is another way – not just for this man, but for those around him. Both he and all the bystanders are encouraged to learn to 'see' differently. Jesus sees him and speaks to him. He is no longer the object of other people's words and suppositions, or the object of their theological musings. He becomes a conversation partner, with dignity and agency. The crowds are invited not just to see *him*, but also to see *themselves*, their callousness, their indifference, their prejudice. As in many miracles of Jesus, 'healing' is not individual. It is a healing of the whole community, and of how the people in that community relate, love and care.

Here, every person is brought into the gaze of Jesus. The hurt and stigmatized, the bystanders, the persecutors. How might it feel to stand in this gaze, and be seen? What part of us may need transformation and healing?

Prayers

Gracious and loving God, who met us in Jesus,
may your gaze rest on us, with healing and challenge,
and bring us into new life.
May you open our eyes that we may recognize stigma and
    prejudice,
and open our mouths that we may bring comfort and
    challenge.
May each and every one of us be brought to see ourselves
    and one another as you see us:
holy, and dearly loved.
In the name of Christ,
Amen

God who sees everything,
I fear your gaze and the gaze of others
and the judgement that may come
on who I am, on my struggles and pain.
Help me receive your gaze
as a gaze of love
from you, who created me,
who knows my struggles,
and comes alongside
to help me bear them.
Amen

Questions to facilitate individual/group study

1 How does your spirituality and that of your Christian faith community speak about pain and suffering? How does it speak of long-term, chronic struggles?
2 Are there people you feel uncomfortable speaking to? Why is that? What words would you use to describe them?
3 Have you ever experienced stigma? What impact has this had on you?
4 How does your church, home group or Christian faith community talk about mental health challenges?
5 What do you think are the essential aspects of 'being human'?
6 What does 'abundant life' look like?
7 What might you be afraid of when it comes to mental health challenges?
8 What does your culture tell you about mental health challenges?
9 How do you think Christians should approach mental health challenges?
10 What kinds of emotions and expressions does your community of faith encourage in the context of worship and prayer?

Pointers to further reading

Goffman, E. (1990), *Stigma: Notes on the management of spoiled identity*, London, Penguin.
Wield, C. (2012), *A Thorn in My Mind: Mental illness, stigma and the Church*, Watford, Instant Apostle.

Chapter references

Goffman, E. (1990), *Stigma: Notes on the management of spoiled identity*, London, Penguin.
Swinton, J. (2020), *Finding Jesus in the Storm: The spiritual lives of Christians with mental health challenges*, Grand Rapids, MI, Eerdmans.

3

God in our struggles: finding resilience

I (Chris) was talking with a therapist who would not describe herself as in any sense religious. As we were discussing some of the more difficult challenges that life has thrown at me, she said: 'Your faith must be a comfort to you?'

My reply made her laugh. 'Yes,' I said, 'but the problem with Christianity is that it also gets you crucified!'

I have reflected since on whether or not this was the best reply. At least its unexpectedness seemed to give her pause for thought. A part of me worries that I might have put her off Christianity, but she has many years' experience of talking to people struggling with the worst that life has thrown at them and it was important to be honest. Christians are not exempt from anxiety, depression, trauma or relational difficulties. Jesus is recorded as saying that his followers must take up their crosses if they wish to follow him (e.g. Mark 8.34). Paul spoke of sharing in the sufferings of Christ (Philippians 3.10) and even of being crucified with Christ (Galatians 2.19). However we understand these passages, they certainly give no support to any idea that Christian life will be easy or free from mental anguish. Why, then, might we ever imagine that things should be any different?

One argument for thinking differently might go something like this. If we believe that God answers prayer, that Jesus brings healing and that life is meant to be lived according to the Creator's plan, people who pray, seek healing and follow God's plan for their lives should find themselves as recipients of divine protection, healing and peace. Conversely, if you find yourself traumatized, anxious or depressed, there must be something wrong. Perhaps you are lacking in faith, or haven't been living according to God's plan or haven't been praying as you should? It all sounds quite convincing, and, very sadly, these are exactly the kinds of arguments that are sometimes used by some Christians to 'comfort' other Christians who are suffering. The impact of such arguments is to further increase the suffering of those to whom they are directed.

Arguments of this kind are very seductive. They seem to offer a Christian life which can be free from the mental and physical suffering that Jesus and his followers experienced, as recorded in the New Testament. They offer an 'easy' answer or, at least, an answer which sounds easy. They appear to be based on faith. In fact, they are none of these things. They are based on a superficial and selective reading of Scripture, a misunderstanding of the nature of faith, and a failure to engage with some of the very real practical challenges of Christian discipleship. This is not to say that miraculous healings do not occur, but rather that they are not something we can take for granted; they are not the norm.

Another argument for thinking differently – for thinking that we can avoid sharing in the sufferings of Christ – might come from a more surprising quarter. There is actually good research to suggest that belonging to a faith community, and following a spiritual or religious way of life, is associated with greater evidence of positive mental wellbeing, and lower rates of most of the common psychiatric disorders. Furthermore, when religious people do suffer from mental disorders such as depression, they seem to make a better response to treatment and recover more quickly. There are also benefits (at least sometimes) associated with incorporating spirituality and religion into mental health treatment programmes. Much, albeit not all, of this research has been undertaken in Christian populations. The scientific evidence thus supports the contention that faith is good for our mental health.

These research findings are very important, and certainly show that we should bring to an end the twentieth-century practice, evident in much of the Western world, of separating our understanding of spirituality, religion and faith from our understanding of mental health. These are not separate areas of life which have no connection with one another. Spirituality is an important part of mental wellbeing, and mental wellbeing cannot be separated from spirituality except at great cost to many patients in mental health services. However, the findings are statistical, not absolute. There are still plenty of Christians struggling with mental health challenges, even if – overall – faith may offer a protective benefit. There may even be some circumstances in which Christians may struggle *more* with their mental health because of their faith. There are aspects of the Christian life which may make some Christians more vulnerable to mental illness, for example because they are persecuted for their faith, or because they struggle to understand why God is allowing bad things to happen to them or their families. These struggles are often a real challenge, both spiritually and psychologically, and we will look at some of them more closely later in this chapter.

At the same time, my therapist friend is right. My Christian faith is a comfort to me, and many others also find that their faith helps them to cope in times of illness, crisis and adversity. Faith is a coping resource, but the ultimate end of faith is to be found in God, not in the avoidance of all suffering. Faith may sometimes alleviate our suffering, but it also helps us to cope in the face of suffering. To use a term that is popular these days in psychological research, faith and Christian spirituality may make us more 'resilient'. However, Christian spirituality does not simply baptize psychological resilience. It gives us cause to radically re-evaluate our understanding of what resilience looks like.

Resilience

The word 'resilience' is used by psychologists in a largely metaphorical way, drawing on its usage in the physical sciences and in engineering. In that context, resilience is usually concerned with what happens under stress – it refers to the ability to bounce back and to return to an original state. When talking about people, it might conjure images from popular films: pictures of Superman or Arnold Schwarzenegger – always bouncing back, no matter what their adversaries throw at them (kryptonite excepted!). Psychological resilience is not normally like that. Human resilience requires the ability to adapt and reconfigure. It includes the possibility of growth – becoming something new and different – in the face of adversity. Human resilience is not about remaining unchanged by stress; in fact, it is often quite the opposite. It is about changing in a way that is adaptive and that facilitates coping when things don't get better.

Even if things do get better, the resilient person may still be for ever changed by what has happened. Resilience is not about going back to how things were before the adversity. This is especially so if the adversity was severe – as it frequently is in the case of mental illness.

Mental illness is often triggered by adverse events, but it is also a kind of adversity in itself. Post-traumatic stress disorder (PTSD), for example, is a mental disorder which is precipitated by exposure to severe or life-threatening events. However, PTSD may continue for months or years after the event. Living with PTSD is stressful, both for the individual concerned and for family, friends and colleagues. Similarly, depression is often triggered by painful life-events, but the experience of living with depression is itself a painful experience, and it often brings as many challenges to Christian faith as any events that caused it. Depression may also arise in the absence of any obviously stressful or difficult circumstances. An experience of severe depression is itself an adverse life-event.

In psychological research, the kinds of factors that have been found to make people more resilient to adversity include such things as:

- realistic optimism;
- facing fear;
- reliance on an inner 'moral compass';
- religion and spirituality;
- social support;
- resilient role models;
- physical fitness;
- brain fitness;
- cognitive/emotional flexibility;
- meaning and purpose in life.

It is important to note that religion and spirituality are on this list because of empirical research which suggests that they are important (Southwick and Charney, 2018), not for any theological reason. Other factors on the list – for example optimism, facing fear, or finding meaning and purpose – may also be a part of a healthy spirituality, even though not explicitly labelled as such. However, there are good theological reasons why Christians (and others) might see their faith as helping them to be resilient. St Paul, for example, talks about how his faith helped him to cope in the midst of affliction:

> Blessed be the God and Father of our Lord Jesus Christ, the Father of mercies and the God of all consolation, who consoles us in all our affliction, so that we may be able to console those who are in any affliction with the consolation with which we ourselves are consoled by God.
> (2 Corinthians 1.3–4)

The 'consolation', or encouragement, that Paul talks about here is actually much richer than the English translation suggests – more like God coming alongside us. The affliction that Paul speaks of here is incurred in the course of his apostolic ministry, but the principle, of a God who comes alongside Christians in times of affliction, is a much broader one. Paul found encouragement in his relationship with God in times of adversity, and so can we. To this extent, his faith was a good psychological coping resource: it sustained him when life was hard. However, faith is much more than this, and the psychological notion of 'resilience' is rather pallid in comparison with the full scope of what Paul has in mind.

Christian resilience

The passage from Paul's second letter to the Corinthians, quoted above, suggests that God comes alongside us in our afflictions not only for our own benefit, but so that we may encourage others as well. When we are feeling anxious, afraid or depressed, we are probably not going to be thinking that we are in any position to encourage others who are feeling the same. However, we can often be much more of an encouragement to others than we may realize, and it is too easily assumed that people struggling with mental disorders are people to be 'ministered to', rather than people who have something to give. Christian resilience is not just about how *I* cope with adversity; it is also about the encouragement that I give to *others* amid their adversity. Very often, this will occur quite naturally, and without the person concerned even being aware of how he or she has helped others. Sometimes, it may be a conscious decision. Mutual help groups (e.g. Alcoholics Anonymous) rely on this principle, sometimes referred to as the 'helper therapy principle'. In helping others who face adversity, I find encouragement amid my own adversity. My helping of others is a part of my own 'therapy'. Such groups are therefore not about 'self-help'; rather, they are about people mutually helping one another. Christian churches, when operating well, are demonstrating a similar kind of mutually supportive resilience.

Resilience of this kind (if 'resilience' is the right word to use) is not about being or feeling strong. Later in the same letter, when talking about the light of the gospel of Jesus Christ that shines in Christian hearts, Paul says that

> we have this treasure in clay jars, so that it may be made clear that this extraordinary power belongs to God and does not come from us. We are afflicted in every way, but not crushed; perplexed, but not driven to despair; persecuted, but not forsaken; struck down, but not destroyed; always carrying in the body the death of Jesus, so that the life of Jesus may also be made visible in our bodies.
> (2 Corinthians 4.7–10)

Christian resilience, then, is not about us being strong or powerful; it is about the extraordinary power that is God's alone. This is where Christian resilience contrasts most strongly with the Superman/Schwarzenegger model of resilience. It also contrasts with the psychological model of resilience outlined above. It is not about 'my' resilience, so much as it is about the resilience of Jesus. It is about the life of Jesus being seen in us, amid adversity, at the same time as we participate in the death of Jesus. Paul writes later in his letter that, as he struggled with a seemingly unanswered prayer, God's answer was: 'My grace is sufficient for you, for power is made perfect in weakness' (2 Corinthians 12.9).

Paul concluded:

> So, I will boast all the more gladly of my weaknesses, so that the power of Christ may dwell in me. Therefore I am content with

weaknesses, insults, hardships, persecutions, and calamities for the sake of Christ; for whenever I am weak, then I am strong.
(2 Corinthians 12.9–10)

Christian resilience is found in the midst of weakness.

Christian coping

One of the problems with the word 'resilience' is that it can sound as though it is something that is either there or not. Superman was able to overcome all the odds because of where he was born and who his parents were. Similarly, we may imagine that either we are born resilient or we are not. Actually, although genetics may play some part, human resilience – and in particular Christian resilience – is not like that. There are lots of things that we can do to make ourselves more (or less) resilient in the face of life's challenges. A related area of research that has been important in understanding why some people deal with adversity better than others is that of psychological coping.

Christians, and others, draw on their faith in a variety of ways when coping with trauma, stress or illness. Psychological research has shown that some of these religious coping methods are positive in nature and are correspondingly positive predictors of health outcomes. These positive coping methods include offering forgiveness, seeking God's support and comfort, collaborating and connecting with God, acting in accordance with what is right, and reappraising what is going on as being for good.

In contrast to positive religious coping, there are other ways of drawing on faith which are negative, both in terms of the way in which they view God and in terms of health outcomes. These include reappraising what is going on in life as evidence of God's punishment, or as the result of demonic activity, and feeling discontent with one's relationship with God and discontent with others (e.g. clergy, other Christians).

Struggling with God

Sometimes, the stress that has to be coped with comes from within Christian faith itself. This can come about in a variety of ways. For example, God may be seen as the cause of the problem, either because he is seen to have allowed unjust suffering, or because he is viewed as disapproving or punishing and thus intentionally inflicting suffering. In these circumstances, the experience of 'struggling with God' may feel like Jacob's experience of wrestling with God (Genesis 32.24–28), as though God is our adversary. Many of the psalms in the Old Testament deal with situations of this kind, from David's sense of guilt over his adultery with Bathsheba (Psalm 51) through to the experience of the wrath of God, and abandonment by God, in Psalm 88.

Another kind of spiritual struggle attributes affliction to supernatural evil. For example, mental illness may be attributed to demonic activity. Such struggles are often associated with Charismatic or Pentecostal churches, but most parts of the Christian Church, to a greater or lesser extent, have some beliefs and practices of this kind. Struggles with what is perceived as demonic may lead to neglect of other dimensions of the problem, as in cases where Christians do not seek medical help when needed because they perceive the problem as requiring a spiritual response (e.g. exorcism or deliverance) rather than a medical one.

Christians also struggle with forgiveness. Generally speaking, the emphasis on forgiveness within Christian teaching would seem to be psychologically helpful. An ability to forgive, and to receive forgiveness, is therapeutic and provides a positive coping response to disharmony with others. However, forgiveness is not easy. In some circumstances it can seem completely impossible. In other situations, if there is pressure to forgive prematurely, or an unrealistic expectation of forgiveness for a major offence committed by someone who is unrepentant, it can be psychologically harmful. It can be a real struggle to forgive someone who has hurt us deeply. At the other extreme, some Christians become preoccupied with very minor (or even imaginary) sins and failings for which they perceive a need for forgiveness. Obsessive concerns of this kind, often referred to as 'scrupulosity', may be associated with obsessive-compulsive disorder.

Sadly, spiritual struggles also result from interpersonal dynamics within Christian communities. Those who should be known by their love for one another (John 13.34–35) not infrequently find themselves struggling with one another. Such conflicts may arise as a result of spiritual abuse, an excessively authoritarian approach to church discipline, perceived disrespect of sincerely held Christian beliefs, a clash between differing interpretations of Scripture (e.g. over issues of sexuality) or even doctrinally sanctioned violence. They may simply arise from flawed human nature, difficulties in communication or personality clashes. Christian Scripture gives reason to believe that such conflicts have always been evident within the community of faith. From Joseph's conflict with his brothers in Genesis, through to disagreements over eating food offered to idols in the New Testament, God's people always seem to have found cause for arguments and disputes with one another.

Christians struggle with God, with forces of evil, with forgiveness and with one another. There are no easy answers to any of these struggles; that is why they are a struggle! However, in general, positive approaches to spiritual coping seem to be better than negative ones, and pastoral responses that seek to integrate a clinical and a spiritual response (e.g. one in which there is collaboration by both health professionals and clergy) are better than those that set up the spiritual and medical dimensions as being in opposition to each other.

The dark night

Struggling spiritually with things that we perceive, with things that are tangibly 'there' (even if invisibly so) – with God, with demons, with other people – is hard enough. Struggling spiritually with what we do not perceive, with what we have lost, with darkness, absence and doubt, can be even harder. For a period of nine months in 1577–8, St John of the Cross, a Carmelite friar, was imprisoned and cruelly treated by members of a different faction of the same order in their monastery in Toledo in Spain. John eventually escaped, at night, and wrote about his experiences, not as a narrative or biography but in the form of a poem, titled 'On a Dark Night' (*En una Noche Oscura*). John later wrote a commentary on the poem, in which he explores the night of faith that ensues when the things that we feel are supportive of faith are withdrawn from us.

John's writings are not an easy read. The poetry is beautiful. It relies on imagery, metaphor and allegory reminiscent of the Song of Songs in the Old Testament, but its meaning is not self-evident. The commentary (in two books, *The Ascent of Mount Carmel* and *The Dark Night*) draws on medieval scholastic theology and assumes a very different understanding of human nature from the one that we adopt today. However, John's experiences have resonated widely with other Christians, and with those from other faith traditions. John challenges us about how we find faith, hope and love amid experiences which seem to deny our faith, preclude hope and resist love. He asks us what we do when the things that comfort us in our faith are withdrawn and when God seems to be absent.

Reference is made not infrequently, by psychiatrists and others, to the ways in which John's dark night, or more correctly dark nights (he describes at least four different varieties of night), resemble depression. In the midst of a depressive illness, a Christian may feel forsaken by God, and may struggle with forms of prayer that no longer seem relevant or helpful. He, or she, may feel like a spiritual failure, may feel discouraged, unworthy, despairing and sad. All of this, the psychiatrist observes, is characteristic of a depressive disorder. Thus, the argument goes, in the light of modern psychological understanding of such things, the dark night is simply another way of talking about the spiritual dimension of depression. Others have seen things differently. They point out, for example, that the person amid a dark night retains a positive approach to relationships with others, can still find hope and meaning, and wishes to recover in a way that the person with a severe depressive condition often does not.

The dark night provides a classic example of the ways in which spiritual and psychological struggles are not easy to disentangle. It is hard to talk about spiritual things without resorting to psychological terms. It is easy to reduce spiritual things (if one is so inclined) to a purely psychological account. In fact, the reality is that the spiritual dimension of life – our experience of relationship with God – involves us as whole people, body, mind and spirit. Some people may be suffering from both a dark night experience *and* depression, while others may be experiencing only one *or* the other. The medical model of differential diagnosis as a way of distinguishing between the two is not helpful here. It may still be important to receive a psychiatric diagnosis, and engage with appropriate treatments, even if one is in the midst of a dark night; the two conditions are not mutually exclusive.

The spiritual challenge is concerned not with diagnosis or pharmacology, but with how faith responds to darkness. Although John would not have used the word, it is about our spiritual 'resilience'. How do we pray when the forms of prayer that we used to enjoy now seem dry and empty to us? How do we believe when God seems absent? John invites us to explore a Christian kind of resilience that is only made visible in darkness, present in absence, and in which we gain what we most desire only by letting go. This understanding of Christian resilience is resonant with the words of Jesus in Mark's Gospel:

> If any want to become my followers, let them deny themselves and take up their cross and follow me. For those who want to save their life will lose it, and those who lose their life for my sake, and for the sake of the gospel, will save it.
> (Mark 8.34–35)

The dark night inverts many of the psychological assumptions about what Christian resilience should look like.

Christian coping resources

Christian spirituality offers many helpful ways of coping with adversity, some of which have already been mentioned in passing. Just a few examples will be explored further here.

Talking to God: prayer

Prayer is so fundamental to Christian life that it is easy to take it for granted. When life is a struggle, Christians pray. Of course they do! Jesus did, St Paul did, and so have countless others since, including such figures as Augustine of Hippo, Benedict of Nursia and his sister Scholastica, Francis of Assisi, Julian of Norwich, Teresa of Avila, John of the Cross, Thomas Cranmer and Teresa of Calcutta. Indeed, the way in which we pray has been shaped and influenced by all of these men and women.

Prayer is so much a part of our lives and our history that we often do not stop to think what it is that we are doing, or why we do it.

We can pray aloud or in silence. Teresa of Avila, who lived in an age when silent prayer could be very controversial, wrote: 'mental prayer in my opinion is nothing else than an intimate sharing between friends; it means taking time frequently to be alone with Him who we know loves us' (Kavanaugh and Rodriguez, 1976, p. 67).

This 'intimate sharing' can be very important in helping to get us through times of anxiety, fear, depression, or other kinds of mental struggle. However, the purpose is not primarily about reducing our anxiety or lifting our mood. As we learn from the Lord's Prayer, and as Jesus demonstrated in Gethsemane, we pray that God's will may be done. We pray also out of love. God is, as Teresa said, the one 'who we know loves us', and we are called above all to love him with all our hearts (Matthew 22.34–40). We pray, then, out of a love of spending time with the one who has first loved us. If we pray primarily out of a desire to get what we want (healing, relief from suffering, an easier life) then we miss the point. However, that is not to say that prayer is not good for us, and it may be good for us for all kinds of spiritual, theological and psychological reasons.

Another wise woman who wrote about prayer was Simone Weil (see Chapter 1) who, also rather controversially, said that: 'Attention, taken to its highest degree, is the same thing as prayer. It presupposes faith and love. Absolutely unmixed attention is prayer' (Weil, 1952, p. 105).

This can be somewhat discouraging for those of us who struggle to maintain the focus of our attention during prayer! However, I don't think that Weil was under any illusion that the giving of our attention, to God and his world, in faith and in love, is anything other than a huge challenge. It is a challenge on which we may even spend our whole lives, and, if we do, then our lives will be well spent. We are constantly distracted, but sometimes the 'distractions' turn out to be the very things that we should be giving our attention to. Sometimes, our anxiety turns out to be God's way of drawing our attention to what really matters to us.

We pray, then, out of love for God and a desire to be with him and to focus our attention on him, not because of what we will get out of it. Prayer is a moving of focus away from our tendency to be self-centred. The paradox is that, when we do this, as research is now demonstrating, it really does seem to be good for us.

There are lots of ways to pray, and some further reading is suggested at the end of this chapter to provide pointers to the diversity and richness of Christian prayer.

Texting God: Lectio Divina

What is the connection, if any, between the Bible and mental health? This is really the subject for another book (such as *The Bible and Mental Health* – see further reading, below) and is much too broad to address comprehensively here. It would be easy to give too big, or too small, a place for the importance of Scripture as a resource for Christian coping. Article six of the Thirty-Nine Articles of the Church of England says that Scripture 'containeth all things necessary to salvation', but does it contain anything helpful for coping with trauma, adversity or mental illness? A part of the problem here is that we have separated faith and mental health in our modern way of thinking, and we need to reunite them.

It is usually not helpful to go to people caught in the midst of illness, bereavement or trauma and engage them in academic theological debate about how and why a good God allows suffering in the world (the question of theodicy). In fact, it is interesting to see how much beside the point many of the traditional theological arguments are (interesting though they may be in the university common room) when you are caught up in the midst of the most painful experiences of life. Among the things that *are* pastorally helpful is an awareness of having a loving presence alongside, whether that is the presence of family members, friends, or God in Christ. Attentiveness also seems to be important in practice and has neurobiological links with emotional regulation. We have already seen that attentiveness is very much what prayer is all about, and in scientific research much of the focus has been on mindfulness, which has a lot of common ground with contemplative prayer. Rather less research has focused on other spiritual practices which foster attentiveness, such as those involved with reading sacred texts. However, there are good theological and scientific reasons to think that spiritual practices involving Scripture, such as Lectio Divina, are helpful.

Lectio Divina is not about Bible study in the normal sense, nor is it about biblical scholarship. Rather, it focuses attention in successively different ways on the affective significance of Scripture at a particular moment in time. An exercise of Lectio Divina based on the same biblical passage at different times and in different circumstances in life will usually have very different outcomes. The four traditional stages, or movements, of Lectio Divina are reading, meditation, prayer and contemplation. In reading, attention is paid to those words or phrases which particularly stand out or catch the attention. In meditation, time is spent reflecting, with the mind, on the significance of these words, and of the passage as a whole, in relation to one's own circumstance. In prayer, a response is offered to God in words, and requests are made for what is perceived as needful in the light of reading. In contemplation, there is silence, and prayer becomes wordless.

Lectio Divina may not be helpful, or even possible, amid major mental illness. However, it provides one way in which the attentiveness that seems to be important to emotional regulation can become focused on divine revelation, and on those things that are 'necessary to salvation'. Lectio Divina helps us to be spiritually, and perhaps also psychologically, more resilient.

Finding meaning: where is God in all of this?

When bad things happen, whether as a result of illness or traumatic events, Christians (and many others) try to make sense of things within the context of their faith. There are many ways of doing this. Ken Pargament, a psychologist who has done much research in this area, suggests that there are positive ways of reappraising the situation which (according to his research) seem to be beneficial for physical and mental health, and for faith. These positive reappraisals include understanding our situation as a part of God's plan, trying to find out what God is teaching us, trying to see how God might be helping us to grow in faith, viewing events as bringing us closer to God and trying to find spiritual benefit amid the difficult situation. These are not easy things to do and, in some circumstances, they raise real spiritual challenges. For example, trying to see your situation as a part of God's plan is very problematic if you have been sexually abused. This easily becomes a negative reappraisal, not a positive one. However, 'God's plan' is one of redemption – which suggests that things were not right in the first place, not that they were exactly what God planned.

55

Even in the worst circumstances, God has things to teach us, wants to help us to grow in faith and wants us to draw closer to him. So, positive reappraisals are helpful, as long as we consider them wisely and carefully and do not allow them to become negative reappraisals in disguise! They lead to people being healthier and less distressed, and feeling closer to God. They help in finding spiritual growth through adverse experiences.

Other ways of reappraising what is going on seem not to be helpful for wellbeing at any level, whether physical, social, emotional or spiritual. This is not to say that they are *never* right (all of them might be in some circumstances) but rather that they tend to have negative outcomes. These include such things as redefining the situation either as God's punishment (e.g. 'My illness is God's way of punishing me for my sins') or due to the devil (e.g. 'Satan made this happen'), or making a negative re-evaluation of faith (e.g. 'God doesn't answer my prayers').

Some readers will quite rightly say that Christian faith is not always about making ourselves feel good. Sometimes the truth is painful. However, there are also theological reasons for thinking that emphasizing God's judgement at the expense of his mercy, attributing too much power to Satan, or losing faith in God's power to act, might be less than helpful. We might think, for example, of Jesus' reappraisal of the situation of the man born blind:

> As [Jesus] walked along, he saw a man blind from birth. His disciples asked him, 'Rabbi, who sinned, this man or his parents, that he was born blind?' Jesus answered, 'Neither this man nor his parents sinned; he was born blind so that God's works might be revealed in him.'
> (John 9.1–3)

This text, from John's Gospel, is challenging. Does God allow people to suffer disability just so that he can 'show off'?! What about people who are not healed? Nevertheless, Jesus appraises the situation in terms of the power and goodness of God, not in terms of human sinfulness or demonic activity. The resilient Christian does likewise.

Christian belonging

An enormous amount of research shows that having good social support from family, friends and community is good for wellbeing. Belonging to the Church, and thus also a church, provides social support in this general sense but also much more. Christian resilience can come from knowing supportive pastors/clergy, asking others to pray, and experiencing the love and concern of other Christians. Taking a more heavenly view, it might also come from awareness of belonging to the one holy, catholic and apostolic Church, a church which transcends time and geography. It might come from awareness that this Church is the body of Christ, and that we are – each of us – an integral part of that body: 'If one member [of the body] suffers, all suffer together with it; if one member is honoured, all rejoice together with it. Now you are the body of Christ and individually members of it' (1 Corinthians 12.26–27). Importantly, we can find strength not only in being prayed for but also in praying for others, not only in receiving spiritual support and comfort but also in offering such support and comfort to others.

Conversely, discontent with others within the community of faith (disagreements, dissatisfaction with the church leaders, feeling abandoned/ignored/rejected) leads people to feel more distressed than previously. Nor are stigma and prejudice absent from Christian churches. Some patients with major mental illness report that they do not receive help from other Christians, or even that the response of their church has made things worse. When this is the Christian reality, we are all the poorer for it.

While it is nice to see research supporting the benefits of belonging to a community of faith, Christians should not be surprised to hear that being part of a loving and neighbourly community is helpful. Jesus talks of love of neighbour as being second only to love of God (e.g. Luke 10.27–37) and urges us to care for others as though we are caring for him (Matthew 25.31–46). St Paul talks about the Church as the 'body' of Christ, within which each of us has a part to play. We are members of one another (Romans 12.5). If one suffers, all suffer; if one has cause for rejoicing, all rejoice (1 Corinthians 12.26–27). Christians are resilient not as individuals, but as members of God's family (Galatians 1.2).

Forgiveness

Forgiveness is not easy. There are 'lite' versions of forgiveness, which look like forgiveness, and avoid much of the trouble associated with it, but they may well be ways of avoiding rather than ways of coping. Research suggests that forgiveness reduces stress and thereby improves health. Conversely, failure to attend to issues of forgiveness is likely to be stressful. This does not mean that it is always possible to forgive. Sometimes, giving attention to forgiveness may be more about a disposition to be more forgiving. In some circumstances there is no immediate possibility of forgiving, and it is important not to rush things, or to be unrealistic, or to feel under pressure to forgive.

Forgiveness is sometimes understood as a decision, and in certain cases this may be all that it is; it may be helpful to decide to forgive someone. However, forgiveness may also be understood as a process, which often takes time, and in cases where the offence has been complex or severe it is usually more helpful to see things this way.

There are different psychological models of how to go about forgiveness. One is known by the acronym REACH (Worthington et al., 2010):

Recalling the hurt
Empathizing with the other person
Altruism – forgiveness is an unselfish gift to the other person
Commitment (to forgiveness)
Holding on (to forgiveness)

Models of forgiveness as a process locate the decision to forgive within a bigger framework. For example, Robert Enright (Enright and Fitzgibbons, 2015), another psychologist who has conducted extensive research on forgiveness, has suggested that the process has four phases, each of which may be broken down into a number of different elements, or 'units', of forgiveness. It is usually best to get professional help with working through the phases of forgiveness, and 'forgiveness therapy' is now recognized as an evidence-based intervention which may be helpful in many different mental disorders.

Forgiveness as a process may take a long time and may need to be revisited as the consequences of what has been done continue to unfold in new situations, or as they are appreciated in new ways. This is perhaps especially so for those who are traumatized in childhood, and who find a new and deeper understanding of what has happened to them, with all its implications, as they grow into adulthood. We can only forgive what we know about, and to the extent that we understand it (emotionally as well as intellectually).

There are some long lists of what forgiveness *is not*. For example, it is not condoning, justifying, forgetting, reconciling, or a quick fix. It is not all about saying 'I forgive you', or accepting what has happened, or moving on – although all of these things can play their part. Forgiveness is not about changing the past, but it *is* about finding a future in which the past no longer has a hold on us.

Anyone reading this chapter who has experienced severe trauma, such as sexual abuse, extreme violence, or the murder of a friend or relative, should seek professional help. People should never feel bad that they do not want to forgive someone who has wounded them in such ways.

Conclusion

Christian resilience is about deriving comfort from faith in times of stress, adversity and illness; it is also about losing our lives to find them, taking up our crosses to follow Jesus. It can be a struggle, but it is about having God *with* us amid our struggles. It can feel as though we have been struggling – wrestling – with God, but then we discover that we have been blessed in the process.

Christian resilience may take many forms. There is evidence that faith does protect people from mental illness, and for those who do suffer illness it may help them to get better more quickly. For others it is more about the long haul, about finding God alongside amid the suffering. For some it is a dark night, where God's presence seems more like absence, and where we have to let go of things in order to gain that which matters most.

Christian resilience thus draws on much of what psychology teaches us about the human capacity to endure adversity, but it is also much more than this. It is paradoxical, looking more like weakness than strength, but always holding on to faith, hope and love. Christian resilience looks like Jesus.

Biblical reflection

But we have this treasure in clay jars, so that it may be made clear that this extraordinary power belongs to God and does not come from us. We are afflicted in every way, but not crushed; perplexed, but not driven to despair; persecuted, but not forsaken; struck down, but not destroyed; always carrying in the body the death of Jesus, so that the life of Jesus may also be made visible in our bodies. For while we live, we are always being given up to death for Jesus' sake, so that the life of Jesus may be made visible in our mortal flesh. So death is at work in us, but life in you.
(2 Corinthians 4.7–12)

The picture of jars of clay is a powerful one. Paul here invites his readers to consider two things: on the one hand, the extraordinary worth of human beings, that they should be recipients of the very life of the Spirit of God; and, on the other hand, human beings' extraordinary fragility. Fragility and glory go together; they are at the very heart of the incarnation, of the story of Jesus, and they are at the heart of what it means to be children of God. You may want to take some time to reflect on these two things. What does it mean to be so precious that God's Spirit dwells in you, that you are loved by the Creator of all things? And how do you feel about the fragility of being human – of having a body, a mind, that can be broken or hurt so easily?

An African Christian once preached on this passage in a UK church and had to explain jars of clay. He said: 'Where I come from in a little village in sub-Saharan Africa, clay pots are everything. They're not special. We don't use them for fancy meals or decoration. We have these huge, giant clay jars, and when it rains, they collect the water. We store water in them. They're not that sturdy – they can crack, and they often need to be repaired or even replaced. But they are our most precious possession. They store water, so they store life. We don't get much rain; water is scarce. Without water, we have nothing. The jars of clay are everything.'

Life wouldn't have been that different in dry parts of the Mediterranean when Paul was writing. He invites his hearers to consider both their worth and the treasure that they hold: the life of God within them, to sustain them and share with others. They do not need to be perfect, or fancy, or even sturdy and unbreakable. They are loved, and the fragility of their nature is also what makes them the best recipients of the treasure of God.

Prayers

God of all people,
who commissioned and loves your Church,
may our churches be places of welcome and mutual
      support;
may we bear one another's burdens
and not add burdens for those who struggle;
may we learn to discern where you work,
even where we do not expect to see you;
may we, as your people,
learn to live abundantly,
even when life itself seems to deny our flourishing.
In the name of Jesus, your Son,
whose life is our life,
Amen

My Lord God,
I have no idea where I am going.
I do not see the road ahead of me.
I cannot know for certain where it will end.
Nor do I really know myself,
and the fact that I think I am following your will
does not mean that I am actually doing so.
But I believe that the desire to please you
does in fact please you.
And I hope I have that desire in all that I am doing.
I hope that I will never do anything apart from that desire.
And I know that if I do this you will lead me by the right
      road,
though I may know nothing about it.
Therefore I will trust you always though

I may seem to be lost and in the shadow of death.
I will not fear, for you are ever with me,
and you will never leave me to face my perils alone.
(Merton, 1958, p. 79)

Questions to facilitate individual/group study

1 How much does your faith bring you comfort in difficult times?
2 Has faith ever been a problem rather than a help? How?
3 What words come to mind when you hear the word 'resilience'? How does this fit with resilience as described in this chapter?
4 What is your most 'comfortable' way to pray? How do you bring concerns into God's presence?
5 What habits or actions do you find helpful for looking after your own wellbeing? Is there anything in this chapter you may want to take up?

Pointers to further reading

Bash, A. (2011), *Just Forgiveness: Exploring the Bible, weighing the issues*, London, SPCK.

Cherry, S. (2012), *Healing Agony: Re-imagining forgiveness*, London, Continuum.

Cook, C. C. H., and I. Hamley (eds) (2020), *The Bible and Mental Health: Towards a biblical theology of mental health*, London, SCM Press.

Enright, R. D., and R. P. Fitzgibbons (2015), *Forgiveness Therapy: An empirical guide for resolving anger and restoring hope*, Washington, DC, American Psychological Association.

Paintner, C. V. (2012), *Lectio Divina, the Sacred Art: Transforming words and images into heart-centered prayer*, London, SPCK.

Pargament, K. I., et al. (1998), 'Patterns of Positive and Negative Religious Coping with Major Life Stressors', *Journal for the Scientific Study of Religion* 37(4), pp. 710–24.

Pritchard, J. (2002), *How to Pray: A practical handbook*, London, SPCK.

Southwick, S. M., and D. S. Charney (eds) (2018), *Resilience: The science of mastering life's greatest challenges*, Cambridge, Cambridge University Press.

White, N. H., and C. C. H. Cook (eds) (2020), *Biblical and Theological Visions of Resilience: Pastoral and clinical insights*, Routledge New

Critical Thinking in Religion, Theology and Biblical Studies, London, Routledge.

Chapter references

Enright, R. D., and R. P. Fitzgibbons (2015), *Forgiveness Therapy: An empirical guide for resolving anger and restoring hope*, Washington, DC, American Psychological Association.

Kavanaugh, K., and O. Rodriguez (1976), *The Collected Works of St Teresa of Avila*, Washington, DC, Institute of Carmelite Studies.

Merton, T. (1958), *Thoughts in Solitude*, New York, NY, Farrar, Straus & Giroux.

Southwick, S. M., and D. S. Charney (eds) (2018), *Resilience: The science of mastering life's greatest challenges*, Cambridge, Cambridge University Press.

Weil, S. (1952), *Gravity and Grace*, London, Routledge & Kegan Paul.

Worthington, E. L., D. J. Jennings and F. A. Diblasio (2010), 'Interventions to Promote Forgiveness in Couple and Family Context: Conceptualization, Review, and Analysis', *Journal of Psychology and Theology* 38(4), pp. 231–45.

4

Recovery from mental health challenges

Allen lived with schizophrenia for many years. His life was filled with alien voices, strange ideas about the world and a general sense that someone somewhere was out to get him. Allen's wasn't an easy life. On the day when he first went to see a psychiatrist, he had already been feeling strange for some time. He was hearing voices and had delusions of being picked on. At one point he became so miserable that he decided he would end his life. His mum encouraged him to seek help. Allen made an appointment to see a psychiatrist at his local mental health hospital. He told her about his experiences and listened intently as the psychiatrist tried to explain: 'Allen, you have schizophrenia. It is a lifelong condition. You will have to take medication for it and indeed you will have to for the rest of your life. But it is manageable, and we can help you.' Allen was shocked. He never really got past the words 'You have schizophrenia'. He, like many of us within society, was terrified by the idea of schizo-phrenia. 'Does that mean I am completely mad?!' Schizophrenia is a heavily stigmatized condition. It is filled with false cultural stereotypes of madness, split personality, violence, danger. Of course, these carica-tures and stereotypes are inaccurate, but that doesn't mean they are not socially powerful in a very negative and damaging way. Allen shared something of the social stigma of schizophrenia and applied it to himself. 'My life is over . . .'

He went home on the bus. He sat down beside a woman whom he had known for some time and told her his story. As soon as she heard the word 'schizophrenia' she stood up and got off the bus. The two never spoke again. Allen made his way home. When he got into his house his mum noticed that he was looking sad. 'What's the matter, Allen?' she asked. Allen told her his story. She looked at him. She smiled. 'Allen, you might have schizophrenia. But you're not a schizophrenic. You are Allen, and I love you.' Allen told me (John) that was a real turning point in his life. He knew he was always going to have to live with schizophrenia. He could accept that as long as he could find hope. His mum gave him the gift of hope. More than that, his mum had reminded him that his name was Allen. People might choose to name him according to his diagnosis, but his mum chose to name him as her son whom she loved (Swinton, 2020, pp. 57–62).

Allen attended a little community in Aberdeen called FRIENDS. FRIENDS was a community of people with lived experience of mental health challenges that met regularly in a local coffee shop within the city. The intention of the community was to offer friendship and support and to enable recovery even in the midst of significant challenges. Each letter of the title FRIENDS (apart from the 'S'!) had a particular meaning:

Friendship
Recovery
Interaction
Enjoyment
Network
Discussion

The main aim of the gathering was to nurture friendship and facilitate recovery. It was there that Allen found friendship, community and a real sense of belonging. He might always live with schizophrenia, but that did not mean he could not flourish in life.

Understanding recovery

Intuitively we might think that recovery means overcoming our mental health challenges and returning to some kind of established norm which doesn't include the distressing experiences that we may previously have had. If I have a chest infection and take antibiotics which get rid of the infection, I might consider myself to have recovered from the infection. Likewise, we might assume that in order to recover from something like schizophrenia, we need to be able to engage in therapy or take medication that will remove the distressing experiences we go through. We would consider ourselves to have recovered when we no longer experience the signs and symptoms of the condition. Allen's story and the aim of FRIENDS suggest that there may be a different way of thinking about recovery. Rather than assuming that recovery has primarily to do with getting rid of distressing experiences (although it can mean this), recovery relates to something slightly different, namely the ability to live a full and meaningful life even in the midst of one's difficulties.

The Mental Health Foundation in the UK points out that recovery can mean different things:

> For some people, it will mean no longer having symptoms of their mental health condition. For others, it will mean managing their symptoms, regaining control of their life and learning new ways to live the life they want. Recovery is often described as a process that isn't always straightforward. You might have days (or weeks, or months) where you feel well and times when your symptoms return. If you've discovered techniques and treatments that work for you, you're likely to feel more confident, and less overwhelmed by your symptoms. When it comes to your recovery, think about what's important for you and what a meaningful life would look like.[6]

The task of recovery is not simply a matter of pharmacological or thera-peutic intervention intended to deal with obvious manifestation of psychological distress (although it may involve such things). Recovery is a personal and relational task within which individuals find ways to achieve their life goals and live meaningful and fruitful lives, as self-defined by criteria that are important to each individual. Recovery means being able to live well, achieve one's own goals, find relationships and live fruitfully even in the midst of difficult experiences. Importantly, recovery is not just an individual thing that people struggle to achieve on their own. Rather, it is a process that involves a wide range of people,

---

6 The Mental Health Foundation (2021), 'Recovery': <www.mentalhealth.org.uk/explore-mental-health/a-z-topics/recovery> (accessed 10 June 2022).

including family, the mental health professions, society, church, and other sources of social and relational support. The recovery process calls for:

> optimism and commitment from people with mental illness, their families, mental health professionals, public health teams, social services and the community. The recovery process is profoundly influenced by people's expectations and attitudes and requires a well-organized system of support from family, friends or professionals. It also requires the mental health system, primary care, public health and social services to embrace new and innovative ways of working.
> (Jacob, 2015, p. 118)

At heart, recovery is a holistic process that looks positively at every aspect of a person's life and seeks to provide opportunities for attaining goals and finding sources of value and hope. The idea of recovery emphasizes that while people may not have control over their symptoms, they can and should have control over their lives. Recovery is thus seen not to be about getting rid of problems, but rather learning to deal with them creatively and holding on to a vision of hope for the future. The recovery agenda is now central to the way in which mental health services are planned in the UK and in most English-speaking countries.

CHIME

In research looking at the factors that were important in recovery (Leamy et al., 2011), as defined by those facing mental health challenges themselves, five recovery processes were identified as particularly important:

Connectedness
Hope
Identity
Meaning
Empowerment

These five factors are referred to by the acronym CHIME. CHIME does not specifically include spirituality, but it is immediately clear that it offers an implicitly spiritual approach to recovery. Spirituality is concerned with human connectedness, with where we find hope and meaning, and with human identity. Spirituality is empowering, not in the sense that it makes us 'powerful', but in the sense that it encourages us to take responsibility for our lives and (as Christians) to draw on God's power, which is made perfect in our weakness (2 Corinthians 12.9).

More will be said about connectedness and relationship in a Christian context later in this chapter, but peer support, relationships and a sense of belonging are all vitally important to recovery. Recovery is not pursued in isolation. At the same time, hope and optimism about the future, belief in the possibility of recovery, and motivation to change, at the individual level, are all important if recovery is to be a positive process of change. As we saw with Allen's story, a positive individual sense of identity is needed, in contrast to a stigmatizing collective identity. Spirituality is particularly important in providing a sense of meaning amid mental health challenges, although understanding this meaning may take a lot of hard work, and it can sometimes be a focus of spiritual struggles (see Chapter 3). Finally, empowerment involves taking personal responsibility and control, and focusing on strengths rather than weaknesses. The disciplines of Christian spirituality – finding God's help in overcoming our vices and growing our virtues, so that we become more like Christ – are focused on exactly this kind of process.

So, Christian spirituality has an important contribution to make to all of the CHIME processes. Putting things the other way round, we might say that the CHIME processes all find their place within Christian spirituality. Christians are, in a sense, all on a journey of recovery in which faith, hope and love play a central role. Faith provides Christians with identity, meaning and empowerment. Hope is one of the CHIME processes. Love is the way in which Christians understand their connectedness with God and neighbour – as summarized by Jesus (Matthew 22.34–40).

Recovery colleges

One interesting initiative that has pushed into this area has been the development of recovery colleges (Shepherd et al., 2017). Alongside the clinical and therapeutic aspects of recovery (diagnosis, medication, counselling), recovery colleges seek to draw on education as a way of enabling recovery. The thinking behind these colleges is that the more people can learn about themselves and the diagnosis they live with, the more able they are to develop positive self-understandings and creative strategies for recovery. Recovery colleges, which are run by mental health organizations and healthcare trusts, are designed to help people develop new knowledge and new tools that can assist in the process of recovery. The emphasis is on the co-production of knowledge and understanding, co-delivery and co-participation, with courses designed and delivered in partnership with people with lived experience of mental health challenges. Experts by experience and experts by training work together to produce an educational experience that not only provides more knowledge but also builds a strong foundation for the process of recovery.

Within the college structure, people learn together with a strong emphasis on strengths, creativity and positivity. Very often, if not always, this includes attention to the part that spirituality plays in recovery. Importantly, recovery colleges provide education that is not available from other educational sources. They therefore offer an important dimension of social capital that is not available in other contexts. Working together with others in this safe educational environment allows people to learn new skills and to expand and develop skills they may already have. Importantly, recovery colleges are not exclusive. They can include service users, family members, friends and anyone else who may be interested. In this way they seek to model inclusion within a society that tends to exclude people with mental health challenges. Of course, this means that they seek to be inclusive, where appropriate, of spirituality from a variety of different faith traditions, and of those who are spiritual but not religious. This is not a place for proselytizing, but it *is* a place for sharing what has worked and what hasn't in support of recovery.

Recovery narratives

Narrative – or storytelling – has become recognized as a key 'technology' of recovery. Unlike other areas of medicine, psychiatry does not have *objective* tests (e.g. for temperature, blood pressure or chemical indicators) that enable a study of the process of 'getting better'. Instead, people struggling with mental health challenges can tell their *subjective* stories of the process of recovery. This storytelling may, in itself, be helpful and healing, although it has also been pointed out by some critics that it has its downside. It can foster a positive sense of identity, a search for meaning, and an understanding of illness and of the strategies that do and do not help in staying well or overcoming setbacks. It can help in developing positive relationships. However, there are questions about whether or not the narratives that are produced reflect real life, especially when they are produced for a particular audience, with perhaps unhelpful expectations about what 'should' be said. Recovery narratives may sometimes be exaggerated, and some people simply do not find storytelling of this kind either easy or helpful.

While these debates will continue, and it is important that they do, for many people, telling the story of their illness and recovery is both personally important and necessary. Such stories emerge from a place of often very deep suffering and vulnerability. Sometimes they have a happy ending, but, more often, in relation to mental health challenges they represent an attempt to explain the chaos and the struggle and the continuing journey. They provide a means of searching for meaning and self-understanding. They may be produced at the request of a health professional, as a part of therapy, or for a group of fellow strugglers who are sharing together their different stories of recovery from mental health challenges, perhaps in a recovery college. They may be written never to be read by anyone else, or perhaps only to be read by an intimate partner or friend, or they may be published for anyone to read.

Christian Scripture contains many narratives, not least those of the Gospel accounts of the life, death and resurrection of Jesus. Christians and Jews have always used narrative as a key tool for doing their theology. Both the Old Testament (the Hebrew Bible) and the New Testament are full of stories. For Christians engaging in recovery from mental health challenges, one of the key tasks is to find how and where their story engages with the wider story of faith. In particular, how does 'my' story of recovery from mental health challenges relate to the story of Jesus, and the story of the Church? This is why Allen's story, and other stories included in this book, are important. They provide examples of how Christians have made sense of their struggles with mental health challenges in the context of their faith, or perhaps how they have struggled to make sense. They tell of how God has been present amid these struggles, or perhaps how God has seemed absent. They are stories of recovery, but they are also stories of being in the same place as Job, or the man blind from birth (John 9), or the woman with a spirit of weakness (Luke 13), or – like St Paul (in 2 Corinthians 12) – finding that your prayers are simply not answered as you would like them to be. They are stories of encounters with God amid human weakness.

The two perspectives that recovery incorporates – the clinical and the personal – are not, and should not be perceived as, incompatible. Both are required for truly holistic care. For both approaches, the overarching intention is to ensure that people live lives that are full and meaningful, even if there is no cure for their ailment. Allen didn't find a cure, but he did find himself as he engaged with those who sought to offer professional care and those friends whom he discovered on his personal journey towards recovery.

Mental health challenges

Before we move on to explore how we might understand recovery theologically, it will be helpful to offer a brief comment on language. As we discussed in the introduction to this book, there is a continuing conversation around how people's mental health issues should be named. Some prefer the term 'mental illness'; others use the term 'mental health problems'. For the purposes of this chapter, we are mainly using the term 'mental health challenges'. People are of course free to name their condition in whatever way they want, and many people prefer the term 'illness'. That is absolutely as it should be. Part of living life in all of its fullness (John 10.10) relates to being able to maintain one's autonomy and to make decisions about one's life, including what one's diagnosis may mean, and how it should be articulated. As we reflect on issues around recovery, the language of mental health challenges encourages us to think positively and hopefully in ways that include the whole community. Similarly, in the work of a recovery college or a mental health clinic, the language of mental illness can be helpful in thinking through how medical resources can assist an individual embarking on recovery from an acute episode of illness.

Rather than thinking that all we can do is wait for rescue (although sometimes that is exactly how we feel and what we have to do), the idea of mental health 'challenges' urges us, with the help of others, to ask the questions: 'What options do I have?' 'How can I get there?' 'What does my future look like? How can I face the future hopefully?' The language of challenges helps move our thinking from helplessness towards recovery. The 'challenge' in 'mental health challenges' is not just for the individual; it is for all of us. Sometimes we might feel that the challenge is just too much, that it is a real struggle; and that is a valid way to feel. But when we feel that way, others need to hold the challenge for us: sit with us, wait with us, struggle with us, continue to love us until we can move towards recovery, even if our steps towards recovery are tiny. In this sense *all of us are responsible for responding to mental health challenges, and all of us are responsible for helping one another to find recovery*.

Health, healing and recovery

With these provisional thoughts around recovery in mind, we can now turn to explore what recovery might look like within the context of the Church. Earlier, we pointed out that recovery should not be equated with curing and/or the eradication of symptoms. The tendency to confuse recovery with cure is something that is often apparent within church communities, particularly around the issue of healing. In the eyes of many, recovery and healing are closely tied together, the assumption being that in order to recover from a mental illness, one must no longer have it. According to this view, the task of the healing ministry is to get rid of the ailment in order that a person can return to 'normal', that is, they can recover. If they do not recover, then the temptation is to try to explain why this is the case: 'You have a lack of faith.' 'You need to pray harder.' 'Read your Bible more. Claim the promises!' This of course simply adds more suffering to the suffering that is already present. The problem seems to be that some people's expectations of the healing ministry are more akin to cultural expectations of medicine than to what the Bible has to say. The language of mental health challenges can help to move us away from such expectations.

Those of us within the Western world live in a highly medicalized context. It is very difficult for us to think about health and ill health without first thinking about medicine. This is rather strange, as most of the healing that goes on in our lives occurs in non-professional contexts at home, in our communities or among friends. The temptation is to assume that our world view is the same as the world view of the first-century Mediterranean culture as it is revealed to us in the Gospels. When we do this, we presume that the stories of healing and recovery that we find in the Gospels equate to biomedical understandings as we conceive of them today. The problem with world views is that we look *through* them, not *at* them. Until someone points out our world view, it is invisible to us. However, if we can get past our world view and look at the world view of the Gospels on its own terms, interesting new possibilities for recovery begin to emerge.

It is worth noting that the Bible does not have a word that is equivalent to a biomedical view of health as the absence of illness. The closest word is the Hebrew term *shalom*, which means peace: peace in the world, peace with the world, peace with other creatures, peace with human beings and ultimately peace with God. The core meaning of shalom is justice, righteousness, right relationship with God. To be healthy is to be in right relationship with God. Everything else springs from this core relationship. This understanding of health stands in tension with some of our assumed norms. Powerful, hedonistic athletes may be deeply unhealthy. Those of us who are on our last legs dying from cancer may be healthy. Within this understanding, even in the midst of the mental health difficulties that we encounter, health remains a possibility. From a Christian perspective, health in general, and mental health in particular, is not the *absence* of symptoms and illness. It is faith in the *presence* of God with us, even in the midst of our greatest struggles.

The psalms of lament provide good examples of what this looks like. Take Psalm 13 for example:

How long, O LORD? Will you forget me for ever?
How long will you hide your face from me?

How long must I bear pain in my soul,
  and have sorrow in my heart all day long?
How long shall my enemy be exalted over me?

Consider and answer me, O LORD my God!
  Give light to my eyes, or I will sleep the sleep of death,
and my enemy will say, 'I have prevailed';
  my foes will rejoice because I am shaken.

But I trusted in your steadfast love;
  my heart shall rejoice in your salvation.
I will sing to the LORD,
  because he has dealt bountifully with me.

The psalmist is in deep suffering and sorrow. He cries out to God. He struggles with the thought that God has forgotten him, hidden from him, deserted him. But then, in the penultimate verse of the psalm, he finds God's *hesed*, God's unending love, which leads him to praise. The key point here is that nothing changes in terms of the reality and presence of the suffering. What has changed is that the psalmist is able to recognize God's unending love in the midst of his suffering and confusion. That recognition didn't take away the suffering, but it did reframe it in a way that introduces hope. The psalms of lament thus provide us with an interesting theological perspective on recovery in the midst of suffering. God may not take away our suffering, but God's presence makes a difference to the challenge that our suffering brings. God's presence offers us hope, companionship and the possibility of something beyond the immediacy of our present distress. God does not offer the psalmist a cure for his woes. But he does offer a mode of companionship and healing.

In the light of this it becomes clear that the goal of spiritually oriented mental health care, which seeks to contribute to the kind of recovery discussed earlier in this chapter, is not simply the eradication of symptoms. Rather, it is a hope that is grounded in faith in God's loving presence. It therefore involves us in helping people to hold on to God's presence at all times and in all circumstances, and especially as they struggle with mental health challenges.

There is of course a danger in this way of reframing health and recovery. Thinking in this way could reinforce spiritually prescriptive antidotes to people's mental health struggles. For example, if we define mental health as 'right relationship with God', people who are struggling with mental health challenges could be viewed as 'not in right relationship with God'. If this happens, the solution to their problems becomes a spiritual one: 'You are experiencing depression or anxiety, so you must be doing something wrong in your relationship with God.' However, the suggestion that mental health relates to shalom is not intended to explain the *origins* or *causes* of particular mental health challenges. It is meant to clarify the *goal* of mental health care and how Christians can be enabled to live well even in the midst of their struggles. Saying, 'You are depressed because you are not in a right relationship with God' – a statement that tries to explain the clinical phenomenon of depression in theological terms – is not the same thing as saying, 'The goal of our mental health care is to help us hold on to Jesus even in the midst of the storms.' One response claims to know the causes of depression without paying attention to the clinical dimensions of depression. The other simply seeks to help people live faithfully in difficult times, a task that requires both spiritual and clinical dimensions. One response is judgmental and pseudo-clinical; the other response is compassionate and faithful to the words of the psalmist:

[God] heals the broken-hearted,
   and binds up their wounds.
(Psalm 147.3)

Healing as connection

If it is the case that health is a movement towards God even amid difficulties, this changes our perspective on what we might mean when we talk about healing and offers a very interesting theological perspective on the Church's contribution to the process of recovery. To begin with, it is helpful to bear in mind the distinction between *curing* and *healing*. The example of the healing of the woman with the discharge of blood in Mark 5.25–34 will help us to see this distinction. The woman makes her way through the crowd and touches Jesus' robe. Immediately she is cured. She then encounters Jesus and confesses what she has done. Jesus says to her: 'Daughter, your faith has made you well; go in peace, and be healed of your disease' (Mark 5.34). This is an unusual statement. Clearly it was the power that went out of Jesus that brought about the physical changes which cured the woman's ailment. True, she believed that Jesus could do something, and he did. It was an act of faith and trust. But why does Jesus then send her to 'be healed of your disease'? Has she not already been cured? Is Jesus speaking of the future or about the past?

Our medicalized Western eyes are naturally drawn to the place in the story where the woman was cured. But there is something else going on here. What if we were to consider the possibility that the healing Jesus is pointing towards is not simply her physical healing, but her *social* healing? If we do that, things begin to look slightly different. Some of the laws of the Pentateuch decreed that blood caused pollution – not moral pollution but pollution that requires separation and cleansing. We are not sure how many people lived by these laws in the time of Jesus, but their effect would have been felt in the culture around, and in how the woman was regarded. The important thing to notice for current purposes is that her condition would have prevented her from being a part of the community. It would have stopped her from going to the Temple and carrying out the ablutions that were assumed necessary to commune with God. In a theocentric community within which someone's personhood is dependent on being a part of the community and being in right relationship with God, this woman was truly perceived as a godless non-person.

As she touched Jesus' robe, everything changed. But the curing was only a first step towards her healing. The miracle has two dimensions. The first is the curing. The second is the healing. Her curing leads to her healing, that is, her reconnection with self, God and community: her return to shalom. This, perhaps, explains Jesus' somewhat mysterious words following her curing: 'Go in peace and be healed of your disease.' In sending her back into the community to be healed, Jesus reconnects her with self, community and God. It seems that the biological changes which touching Jesus' cloak brought about were not enough in themselves to bring about healing. It was as the woman met Jesus, and as Jesus pointed her towards the source of her relational personhood in God, community and Temple, that the healing was completed.

Does this then mean that she had to be cured in order to be healed? The answer is in the story. She touches Jesus' robe. Immediately Jesus becomes polluted. Jesus, who (as Mark told us in the very first verse of his Gospel) is the Son of God, finds himself polluted and, according to the understanding of the day, unable to commune with God and others. He becomes a godless non-person. In a kind of prefiguration of the cross, we find Jesus taking upon himself the pollution of the woman in order that she can be not only cured but also healed. Importantly, in taking the pollution upon himself he dispels the very idea that human ailments are a blockage to God. The beloved Son of God (Mark 1.11) cannot be alienated from God; Jesus cannot be separated from God. So, in this story, we find Jesus doing away with the old ways and hustling in a new way of thinking about what we need to do to relate to God: nothing.

None of this should be taken to negate the very real sense of separation from God that Jesus does eventually experience on the cross (Mark 15.34). This also can be an experience amid the challenges presented by mental illness – an experience of separation that is a very real sharing in the sufferings of Christ. However, Jesus is eventually vindicated by the resurrection and so – amid our mental health challenges – our faith in God's presence is not invalidated by such experiences. Christian hope is founded on faith, even when faith itself is darkness.

The Church as a community of healing and recovery

If healing is to be understood as connection, this has important implications for the Church as it seeks to minister faithfully to and with people living with mental health challenges as they journey towards recovery. By the term 'Church' we mean here the community of the friends of Jesus. In John 15.15 Jesus tells his disciples that he will no longer call them servants. Now he calls them friends. Friends of Jesus. Jesus sat with and befriended outsiders, tax collectors, sinners, prostitutes, people whom society framed in the negative, and he offered them life-bringing friendship. This is no small thing. Friendship is a critical source of value. How do we gain value, and experience being valued? We can't buy value or whip it up on our own. Value is always a gift. Friendship is a particular form in which the gift of value is given. When Jesus changes the identity of his disciples from servants to friends, he creates a gift-giving community – a community that is called to offer and receive Christ-like friendship. Mental health challenges are culturally devalued human experiences. In a world that worships intellect and reason and assumes that happiness is the meaning of life, it is difficult to have a condition that challenges any one of these cultural values. Friends value one another irrespective of circumstances. They stick by one another amid their struggles. Jesus offers friendship to the outcast, touches those whom society assumes to be unclean, sees people when everyone else simply passes them by (John 5.6). Jesus offers friendship and new life to prostitutes, tax collectors and sinners (Matthew 9.10–17). It's not that he doesn't notice people's problems. He just doesn't begin there.

It is this kind of Christ-like friendship that sits at the heart of Jesus' proclamation: 'I came that they may have life, and have it abundantly' (John 10.10). Life in all of its fullness is a life lived in peace with Jesus, within which hope, promise and life in loving community, both in the present and in the future, become the focus for the goals of our lives. Life in all of its fullness is abundant life. Abundant life is not life without suffering. Rather, it is a life full of joy (John 15.11). It is in the simplicity of the gift of friendship that the Church can offer something profound and often missing from people's lives and in so doing help them move towards the kind of recovery we have been discussing in this chapter.

Conclusion

We opened this chapter with Allen's story. It is fitting that we return to that story as we conclude the chapter. We saw that the possibility of hope for Allen came when he realized the power of his mother's love. This gave him the strength and the encouragement to look at himself differently – to move beyond his self-stigmatization towards the possibility that he could recover and make something of his life. His involvement with the FRIENDS community brought about healing and connection and helped him to find himself in the midst of a community of belonging. The friendships offered by that community gave him value, purpose, hope and joy. His love for Jesus gave him a heavenly hope that guided him through to the end of his days. As I (John) sat at his funeral, some years later, and looked around at the packed congregation, it was clear that Allen wasn't 'just a schizophrenic'. He was Allen, and many people loved him.

Biblical reflection

[Elijah] went a day's journey into the wilderness, and came and sat down under a solitary broom tree. He asked that he might die: 'It is enough; now, O LORD, take away my life, for I am no better than my ancestors.' Then he lay down under the broom tree and fell asleep. Suddenly an angel touched him and said to him, 'Get up and eat.' He looked, and there at his head was a cake baked on hot stones, and a jar of water. He ate and drank, and lay down again. The angel of the LORD came a second time, touched him, and said, 'Get up and eat, otherwise the journey will be too much for you.' He got up, and ate and drank; then he went in the strength of that food for forty days and forty nights to Horeb the mount of God. At that place he came to a cave, and spent the night there.

Then the word of the LORD came to him, saying, 'What are you doing here, Elijah?' He answered, 'I have been very zealous for the LORD, the God of hosts; for the Israelites have forsaken your covenant, thrown down your altars, and killed your prophets with the sword. I alone am left, and they are seeking my life, to take it away.'

He said, 'Go out and stand on the mountain before the LORD, for the LORD is about to pass by.' Now there was a great wind, so strong that it was splitting mountains and breaking rocks in pieces before the LORD, but the LORD was not in the wind; and after the wind an earthquake, but the LORD was not in the earthquake; and after the earthquake a fire, but the LORD was not in the fire; and after the fire a sound of sheer silence. When Elijah heard it, he wrapped his face in his mantle and went out and stood at the entrance of the cave.
(1 Kings 19.4–13)

Elijah is one of the best-known prophets of the Old Testament. He is known for the way he confronted corrupt political rulers and their cronies. Just before this reading, Elijah had defeated the prophets of Baal in a great show of faith and power from God. But here, he is diminished, exhausted and terrified. He begs to die.

It is a story we often tell too fast. We might read of his great victory and think: why on earth does he feel so down? Does he not realize that God is with him? But circumstances do not always match feelings. Elijah's trouble goes deeper than mere response to circumstances. It cannot be solved simply by making his environment 'better'.

Nor can it be solved fast, or in ways that are straightforward. Read the passage slowly and reflect on the different stages Elijah goes through. Time passes. Days of exhausted, burnt-out solitude. God cares for Elijah but does not jump to 'healing' or 'fixing' him. Elijah is given space. He is cared for in terms of his body, his whole person. He is given time. He is not told to snap out of it; God does not argue or try to convince him that his reaction is irrational.

Elijah journeys with a God he cannot see or perceive. And finally, God comes, when Elijah is ready to connect. God does not force presence, encounter or dialogue earlier. God patiently waits for Elijah to be ready.

And at the same time, God acts in strange ways. Readers may expect that what Elijah needed was a show of power, for reassurance: a great wind, or an earthquake. But where Elijah meets God is not the show of power, but the gentle, caring presence that makes space for Elijah himself. And in that space, shalom becomes possible – even if nothing else, ultimately, changes.

Prayers

A prayer for recovery

Gentle and loving God,
when the road is dark and hope seems far away,
may you draw near, in stillness and quiet.
May you help us recognize your still, small voice
and look for you in unexpected places.
When hope has fled and recovery is elusive,
may we find that you yourself are walking with us
in the midst of the storm,

ready to lead us to new, unexpected places.
Amen

A prayer for communities

God of shalom, of peace and justice,
may this place and these people
be bearers of peace.
May this community welcome all who struggle,
accepting them as members of the same body,
with love and honour
and readiness to listen
for what we may learn together
about you and one another.
In the name of Jesus,
Amen

Questions to facilitate individual/group study

1 What do you hear when you hear the word 'schizophrenia'? Or, more widely, 'mental illness'?
2 This chapter redefines what 'recovery' might look like; how do you feel about this redefinition?
3 The acronym CHIME (Connectedness, Hope, Identity, Meaning, Empowerment) offers five crucial factors in recovery. How does this fit in with what you might have observed in your life and those of others?
4 How helpful do you find it to talk about mental health challenges rather than mental illness? What do you find helpful or unhelpful about different language such as 'mental health', 'wellbeing', 'mental health challenges' and 'mental illness'?
5 What does 'living faithfully in the midst of difficult times' look like for you?
6 How could your faith community improve its involvement in supporting recovery from mental health challenges?
7 'Mental health challenges are culturally devalued human experiences.' How could this change? How might you and your community tell stories in a way that challenges this devaluing?

8 What can church congregations learn from Christians who are in recovery from mental health challenges?

Pointers to further reading

Care Services Improvement Partnership et al. (2007), *A Common Purpose: Recovery in future mental health services*, London, Social Care Institute for Excellence.

Cook, C. C. H. (2016), 'Narrative in Psychiatry, Theology and Spirituality', in C. C. H. Cook, A. Powell and A. Sims (eds), *Spirituality and Narrative in Psychiatric Practice: Stories of mind and soul*, London, RCPsych Publications, pp. 1–13.

Leamy, M., et al. (2011), 'Conceptual Framework for Personal Recovery in Mental Health: Systematic Review and Narrative Synthesis', *British Journal of Psychiatry* 199(6), pp. 445–52.

Swinton, J. (2020), *Finding Jesus in the Storm: The spiritual lives of Christians with mental health challenges*, Grand Rapids, MI, Eerdmans.

Chapter references

Jacob, K. S. (2015), 'Recovery Model of Mental Illness: A Complementary Approach to Psychiatric Care', *Indian Journal of Psychological Medicine* 37, pp. 117–19.

Leamy, M., V. Bird, C. Le Boutillier, J. Williams and M. Slade (2011), 'Conceptual Framework for Personal Recovery in Mental Health: Systematic Review and Narrative Synthesis', *British Journal of Psychiatry* 199(6), pp. 445–52.

Shepherd, G., J. McGregor, S. Meddings and W. Roeg (2017), 'Recovery Colleges and Co-Production', in M. Slade, L. G. Oades and A. Jarden (eds), *Wellbeing, Recovery and Mental Health*, Cambridge, Cambridge University Press, pp. 181–93.

Swinton, J. (2020), *Finding Jesus in the Storm: The spiritual lives of Christians with mental health challenges*, Grand Rapids, MI, Eerdmans.

5

Mental health and disability: recognizing limits

Questions around mental illness, mental health challenges, and disability are important but also contentious. Some people are happy to accept the description of their experiences as being a disability. Others are not.

The World Health Organization (WHO) informs us that depression is a leading cause of disability worldwide and a major contributor to the overall global burden of disease.[7] The Pan American Health Organization (PAHO) states: 'Mental health problems are the single largest cause of disabilities in the world.'[8] This seems straightforward, but it is important to be clear about exactly what these organizations mean when they use the term 'disability'. Mental illnesses, like other health conditions, can be disabling insofar as they put limits on what we can do and sometimes prevent us from doing the things that we would like to do. However, over recent years, there has been a move away from a medical model of disability to an understanding of disability as (to a degree) a social construction concerned with norms and expectations which create an unfavourable physical, psychological and social environment. While the medical and social models of disability are often seen as opposed to each other, disability is actually a product of both.

A further problem in discussing mental health and disability is that some people who live with mental health challenges do not want to have the label 'disabled', partly because they simply don't want yet another label and partly because they do not necessarily see themselves as

---

7 World Health Organization (2021), 'Depression': <https://www.who.int/news-room/fact-sheets/detail/depression> (accessed 28 June 2022).

8 Pan American Health Organization (2019), 'Mental Health Problems Are the Leading Cause of Disability Worldwide, Say Experts at PAHO Directing Council Side Event': <https://www3.paho.org/hq/index.php?option=com_content&view=article&id=15481> (accessed 11 June 2022).

disabled. If it is not carefully used, the term 'disability' can quite easily become another source of stigma for people who are already highly stigmatized. However, as we discussed in Chapter 2, stigma is a spoiled identity, an injustice, which sees people as less than what they truly are. This is just as true for people who are disabled as for those struggling with mental health challenges. It is not helpful if one stigmatized group seeks to distance itself from another simply from fear of further prejudice, thus reinforcing the stigma in the process. Nevertheless, the imposition of the term 'disability' on people who feel it is inappropriate is equally unhelpful. Striking the balance between personal choice and communal wellbeing is complex but vital.

In this chapter we will explore the meaning and implications of the term 'disability' and offer some thoughts as to how we might go about understanding the term constructively and creatively in relation to mental health challenges. In exploring the issue of disability, it will be helpful to begin by asking the question: 'What exactly do we mean when we call someone disabled?'

What is disability?

The World Health Organization lays out its definition of disability in the International Classification of Functioning, Disability and Health (ICF). The ICF, which was developed collaboratively by people with disabilities working together with academics and clinicians, defines disability as 'an umbrella term for impairments, activity limitations and participation restrictions. It denotes the negative aspects of the interaction between a person's health condition(s) and that individual's contextual factors (environmental and personal factors).'[9]

So, first, disability is an 'umbrella term' which includes three elements: impairments, activity limitations and participation restrictions. We need to consider each of these in turn.

1 **Impairments** are defined by the WHO as 'problems in body function and structure such as significant deviation or loss'. Although it may

---

9   <www.cdc.gov/nchs/data/icd/icfoverview_finalforwho10sept.pdf> (accessed 15 July 2022).

not be clear from the definition, this includes mental functions, and the ICF has a principle of parity and neutrality: 'In classifying functioning and disability, there is not an explicit or implicit distinction between different health conditions, whether "mental" or "physical". Impairments are the physical or psychological difficulties that people experience. For example, these might include the deep lows of depression, the extreme highs of bipolar disorder, or the obsessional behaviour that sometimes accompanies anxiety disorders. They might include memory problems associated with dementia or with severe depression. It is important to notice that impairments are not in and of themselves necessarily negative. For example, not everyone who hears voices necessarily perceives this as a negative thing. Many people live happily with voices (Hearing Voices Network, 2022).[10]

2 **Activity limitations** are defined by the WHO as 'difficulties an individual may have in executing activities'. These may include such things as learning (e.g. in dementia), communication (e.g. for someone who is depressed), self-care (e.g. for those with eating disorders) or social interactions (e.g. in social phobias). Problems with emotional regulation (an impairment commonly experienced in depression or in anxiety disorders) may make it particularly difficult to handle stress.

3 **Participation restrictions** are defined as 'problems an individual may experience in involvement in life situations' and may involve any area of life, for example discrimination in employment or restricted social relationships.

Second, disability is concerned with a negative interaction between a health condition and the social/environmental context. Impairments and activity limitations do not inevitably cause participation restrictions. The problem is very often the response of others and of society to the individual's impairments. Problems arise due to the negative, interactive social processes that occur when a particular impairment rubs up against social and environmental factors. For example, stigma (which we discussed in

---

10 For more information on the positive dimensions of hearing voices, see the Hearing Voices Network: For people who hear voices, see visions or have other unusual perceptions: <www.hearing-voices.org> (accessed 27 June 2022).

Chapter 2) is deeply disabling. It causes people to look *through* people rather than look *at* them, and reduces them to the size and the social connotations of their diagnosis. The disability that is caused by stigma is not simply related to what is going on within the life of an individual. It has to do with the assumptions made about what other people's lives are like, and the implicit or explicit negative characterization of another person or his or her experience.

Disability is therefore not something that has to do only with what goes on within an individual's life. It is something that happens in the interaction between a health condition and the social and physical environment. When mental health challenges are understood in this way, we can, at one level, say that they are disabling even if they may not be viewed by an individual as a disability.

Mental health disability in lived experience

Judith is a Christian woman who has lived for many years now with a diagnosis of schizophrenia. Whether directly or indirectly, her condition has prevented her from holding down paid employment, but she is very busy in a voluntary capacity working for her local National Health Service (NHS) trust. I (Chris) asked her if she considered herself to be disabled, and this was her reply:

Ironically, I do not consider the more serious aspects of my illness make me disabled. I think there are three reasons for this:

1 It fluctuates so it is not there all the time.
2 When it happens, part of it involves blaming myself for what is happening, so I do not really consider it to be an 'illness' at the time.
3 Self-stigma – over many years I have internalized shame and failure. Thus, I want to almost deny that it has happened, not just to others, but especially to myself. I try not to think about it when things improve.

Of course, when things do get bad, I am temporarily unable to function and need help. I know I should try and avoid stress to

86

decrease the frequency of relapses, but quite often I carry on regardless until the worst happens.

I am mildly disabled due to anxiety, panic and a bad reaction to any form of stress. Especially impactful is social anxiety. I try to limit my activities to minimize this – I know better now what I can cope with.

I am also mildly disabled due to side effects of long-term medication:

- Physically lethargic, especially in the mornings, I struggle to get going.
- Discomfort from constipation can be very severe.
- Unsteadiness – I have had several falls recently.
- I have what I call 'concrete head', when I feel fuzzy and muddle-headed, especially in the morning.

So, overall – yes, I am mildly disabled, but not quite in the way you might think! I regard myself as very fortunate that I can mostly manage to do what I want to do and have so many opportunities. My biggest issue is regretting that I wasted so many years before I discovered them!

Disability in relation to mental health is, as Judith so clearly explains, complicated. Impairments and activity limitations are multiple and various, even in relation to one diagnosis. Judith does not mention her inability to hold down paid employment within her own assessment of her disability. Aspects of the social environment – especially stigma – have become internalized and are now entangled with some of the spiritual challenges that she faces – shame, a sense of failure, and regrets about the past. Judith says that she is 'mildly' disabled, and she achieves an enormous amount despite the impact on her life of a major mental illness and an adverse social context, but some who know her might say that this looks like a very severe disability minimized by the spiritual virtues of courage, faith and patience. Judith has learned to live within limits, but she has also broken out of these limitations and found new vocational opportunities because of, not despite, her disability.

Prejudice and discrimination

A good example of the way in which societal attitudes serve to disable people with mental health problems is in the issue of *prejudice* and *discrimination*. To be prejudiced in any given situation, we must enter into that situation with negative preconceived ideas about what we expect to see and how we expect people to behave. Instead of judging the person or the situation according to its merits, we work on preconceived ideas which may or may not be accurate.

One of the interesting things about human communication is that we all must be mind readers. In order for me to work out how to respond when I am with you, I need to be able to 'read your mind', that is, use the information I think I have about you, combined with the information I gather when I see or hear you, in order to make a judgement on how to behave and respond. Before I can make such assumptions, I need to know certain things about 'normal' communication and gauge something about you from what I know about other people who may be similar to you. So, for example, I might look at you and see that you are wearing a hijab. This would indicate that you are a Muslim, and I would shape my behaviour accordingly. This is a necessary communicational skill.

The problem comes when the information that we receive about other people is profoundly negative. For example, if I am talking to you while working with a caricature of people living with schizophrenia, I may assume that you are violent, have a split personality, are crazy, don't like relationships and so on. Or if I am a Christian, at least in some churches, I might assume you are demon-possessed or lacking in faith. None of these assumptions are true, of course, but if I allow what I pick up from the media, films, society or poor theology to determine my perceptions of people with this particular mental health challenge, then as soon as I hear the term 'schizophrenia' I will immediately lock into my cultural stereotypes. When this happens, I become prejudiced and act in ways that are driven by that prejudice. This leads to discriminatory practices and the further alienation of people who are already struggling with life.

'Prejudice' and 'discrimination' are connected but different terms. Prejudice relates to negative preconceived ideas. Discrimination emerges from prejudice and has to do with unfair actions against a particular individual or group of people. It is clear from the research literature and from the narratives of people with mental health challenges that both prejudice and discrimination are widespread. A recent survey revealed that 88 per cent of the people surveyed felt that discrimination was still widespread.[11] Discrimination worked itself out in several ways:

1 *Directly.* A person experiences discrimination as a direct result of his or her condition. For example, someone with bipolar disorder who is seeking a loan is turned down on the basis that 'people with bipolar disorder are unreliable.'

2 *Indirectly.* Here a general rule that applies to everyone disadvantages someone with a mental health challenge. For example, someone with anxiety and irritable bowel syndrome is disadvantaged in the workplace by a general rule that employees are not allowed to go to the toilet more than three times per shift.

3 *Arising from disability.* You are treated unfavourably because of your mental health condition. For example, someone on heavy medication may find it difficult to get up in the morning. If the employer is unsympathetic, it will be difficult for that person to hold down a job.

4 *Arising from harassment and victimization.* When others are aggressive or derogatory towards a person because of his or her disability. For example: 'Malia has paranoid schizophrenia and works in an office. Two of her colleagues call Malia "schizo" and draw and write abusive words and pictures on her desk. Malia tells her employer about this, who ignores the situation.'[12]

The thing for us to notice here is that none of these disabling experiences emerge directly from the clinical dimensions of the individual's experience. Exclusion and misnaming are not clinical phenomena. They are the consequence of a disabling culture that is prejudiced against

11 Rethink Mental Illness (2021), 'Overwhelming Majority of People Severely Affected by Mental Illness Report Discrimination Still Widespread': <www.rethink.org/news-and-stories/news/2021/05/new-survey-reveals-overwhelming-majority-88-of-people-severely-affected-by-mental-illness-report-discrimination-still-widespread> (accessed 27 June 2022).

12 Rethink Mental Illness (2013, updated 2017), 'Discrimination and Mental Health': <www.ed4health.co.uk/wp-content/uploads/2018/12/Discrimination-_And-_Mental-_Health-_Equality-_Act-Factsheet.pdf> (accessed 28 June 2022).

people with mental health challenges and discriminates accordingly. This is why protective legislation such as the Equalities Act, combined with advocacy and self-advocacy to ensure justice and fairness, is so important at a societal level.

In the light of these rather disturbing observations, we might expect that the Church would be a safe haven for people with mental health challenges. Sadly, church communities can be equally as disabling, prejudiced and discriminating as wider society.

Disabling theologies

Alice is 30 and lives with enduring schizophrenia (Swinton, 2020, pp. 122–3, 151–8). She is a committed Christian. But there are problems:

And one that is really difficult to make when you're talking about being able to see dark figures on people's shoulders, you know? And people go 'ooh demons!' and it's like, potentially, yes, but, you know, what do you do with the good stuff? That's not necessarily demonic that could be Jesus, you know . . . what's going on? So, it's a difficult one. So I had a lot of prayer from very well-intentioned people, about demonic stuff and told that I didn't have enough faith so I wasn't being healed, all that kind of crap that you hear at churches. All the time, it makes me so angry! But it's hard being told that you're filled with evil, you know? Or that everything that you're hearing and seeing is of the devil. Particularly as some of that stuff actually brings you peace. That's really hard. And so to have, I told someone once in a moment of weakness about my girlfriend who would hang out with me in my sad moments, and they said 'oh she's a demon Alice, you shouldn't talk to her.' And I'm like 'she's the only person who sticks around long enough to see me cry.' I'm like, where are you? If there were a real person there maybe I wouldn't need her, would I? So what are you going to do? So yeah it is really difficult when people say that, it is hard (Swinton, 2017, original research transcript).

What might be going on here? People don't like strangeness. It scares them. The best way to control strangeness and fear is to name it – to

90

categorize it in such a way that you can control it. The way we name things is determined by what we think we are looking at. For some Christians a situation like Alice's is frightening and alien. In response they reach into their interpretations of their own tradition and try to name Alice's experiences in a way that will enable control and allow them to 'do something'. The fact that the explanation offered is devastating to the person who receives it is often not considered. How must it feel to be told that the devil is living inside you? Ironically, if Alice had said the same thing to her friend, it would have been assumed to have been a manifestation of psychosis. The problem is that the theology which lies behind the ascribing of this explanation is significantly flawed and, as such, is deeply disabling.

While this kind of negative ascription of the demonic to people with mental health challenges is not uncommon in churches, it is far from common in the Gospels. When we look at the accounts of the demonic in the New Testament, two things quickly become clear. First, many of the demonic encounters relate to physical conditions. In contrast, in churches today we do not normally ascribe the demonic to people experiencing physical illness. The fact people ascribe it to mental health issues may indicate an implicit dualism wherein things that happen to the body are assumed to be physical, but things that happen to the mind are somehow different, more spiritual. This, combined with people's fear of what they do not understand, leads to a potentially toxic situation.

A few years ago, Brian (not his real name) died by suicide. The first reaction of some of his friends was to be concerned with his eternal salvation. They held strongly to the belief that if people take their own life they will miss out on eternal glory. However, following the post-mortem it was discovered that his brain had a significant physical lesion that possibly lay behind the depression that led to his demise. His friends were palpably relieved. In locating the problem in the physical rather than the psychological, they were able to appease their theological concerns. It seems that Paul's words that *nothing* can separate us from the love of God were not enough to allay their fears:

For I am convinced that neither death, nor life, nor angels, nor rulers, nor things present, nor things to come, nor powers, nor

height, nor depth, nor anything else in all creation, will be able to separate us from the love of God in Christ Jesus our Lord.
(Romans 8.38–39)

It would pay us well to be more careful and more biblical when it comes to theologizing about anyone's eternal destiny.

The problem of the demonic

Likewise, and very importantly, the descriptions of the demonic that we find in the Gospels are simply not the same as the accounts of mental disorders that we find in the DSM or the ICD diagnostic criteria. Take for example the DSM's description of schizophrenia which, as we saw, was Alice's diagnosis. Criterion A lists the five key features of psychotic disorders: 1) delusions, 2) hallucinations, 3) disorganized speech, 4) disorganized or catatonic behaviour, and 5) negative symptoms. In DSM-5, two or more of these five criteria must be met in order to make a diagnosis (American Psychiatric Association, 2013, p. 99). Now compare this with the accounts of the demonic in the Gospels. The demons are not delusional. They know exactly who Jesus is, and they are terrified of him. The demon-possessed people do not seem to hallucinate. The people in Scripture who see unusual things seem to be soothsayers and prophets (Cook, 2018, pp. 66–73), that is, people who claim to be in touch with God. Indeed, Jesus hears voices on occasion (Mark 1.11). There is no indication that the demon-possessed are disorganized. They seem to be well organized – by the devil. They are not confused about Jesus. In one case (Mark 5.1–20), they engage in a well-thought-through dialogue without any signs of confusion or cognitive dissonance. Likewise, there is no indication of catatonic behaviour or negative symptoms. It is clear that the Gospels are not talking about the same thing as the person who said that Alice's girlfriend was a demon.

So why do Christians choose to ascribe the demonic to vulnerable people going through difficult times, and not to ascribe it to the things that go on in the political and economic realms of the world – what Paul describes as the powers and principalities (Ephesians 6.12)? The answer is that our imagination around the demonic tends to be more shaped by images from Hollywood than by the story that emerges from Galilee. We gather cultural images of what we think the demonic is and then project them onto experiences of people who make us feel uneasy. If we can name something, we can control it, even if that naming is devastating for the individual who receives the name. It is this kind of disabling theology that disability theology pushes against. Disabling theology leads to disabling attitudes, which in turn lead to alienation, loneliness, self-stigma and a breach in life in all of its fullness. It matters what we believe, but we need to be very careful about where we get our beliefs from. We need to develop a mental health hermeneutic – a way of interpreting Scripture that takes seriously the challenges of human communication and the experience of mental health challenges. This approach can help us to see the pitfalls of inaccurately ascribing things to people that are simply missing from Scripture. But what might that look like?

A mental health hermeneutic

Coreen is 24 and lives with enduring depression. 'Depression' is a term that we use widely – so much so that we forget just how difficult the experience is:

> My normal, the point where I think that everything is more or less normal, you know, when I know that God is still with me, is kind of weird. Depression is a wee bit like an abyss. You know a deep dark pit that you can't ever get out of. So, you have to sit there and just wait. When I'm in there I need medication. It sometimes lifts me up and out of the pit and eventually I get to the point where I can cope, and I am able to be normal. That is great! But it is always like this very tentative kind of healing, very much like you're on this very, very fragile ground. So, when I'm ill I'm in the pit. But when I am well I imagine myself sitting on the edge of the abyss, knowing that I could tumble in at any time. So, my normal is probably not like your normal (laughs).
> (Swinton, 2020, pp. 91–2)

One might expect Coreen's situation to attract compassion. However, her general experience has been mixed. Some people are compassionate. But others seem more interested in trying to use their theological positioning to *explain* her circumstances: 'You need to pray harder!' 'Christians are supposed to be happy. What have you done wrong?' This of course is no help at all and simply adds another layer of disablement to an already disabling condition. What might Coreen's situation look like if we applied our developing mental health hermeneutic to the issue of depression?

We might begin by asking what the Bible has to say about the experience of darkness and lost connection that often marks the lives of Christians living with depression.

The first thing to notice is that when Paul lays out the fruits of the Spirit in Galatians 5.22–23, he does not list happiness as one of the gifts: 'The fruit of the Spirit is love, joy, peace, patience, kindness, generosity, faithfulness, gentleness, and self-control.' It is not difficult to be tempted to equate happiness with faith. 'If I am happy, then I am in a right relationship with God. If I am not happy, then I have a faith problem.' But Scripture does not say that. Happiness may be something we desire, but it is not an enduring emotion; it comes and it goes. The presence of God is not demonstrated by the happiness of God's people. But what exactly do we mean by the presence of God?

Second, we need to ask some tough questions about experiences of the presence and absence of God. At one level it seems obvious that God is always present with us. The writer of Deuteronomy states: 'Because the LORD your God is a merciful God, he will neither abandon you nor destroy you; he will not forget the covenant with your ancestors that he swore to them' (Deuteronomy 4.31). The writer to the Hebrews makes a similar point: 'Keep your lives free from the love of money, and be content with what you have; for he has said, "I will never leave you or forsake you"' (Hebrews 13.5). This seems quite straightforward: *God will never leave us.* And yet Isaiah says this:

> Truly, you are a God who hides himself,
> O God of Israel, the Saviour.
> (Isaiah 45.15)

How can God be present and hiding at the same time? The situation becomes even more complex when we turn to the cross. On the cross

Jesus cries, 'My God, my God, why have you forsaken me?' (Matthew 27.46). How can Jesus, who is God, be forsaken by God? These are difficult questions! There is, however, a way of thinking about them that can help us make sense of the darkness of depression and pull us away from disabling theological assumptions.

In the Old Testament, the psalms of lament present a language for suffering and a way of worshipping even in the midst of suffering. However, not all of the lament psalms resolve in worship. Psalm 88, after describing the struggles of the psalmist with life, and with a sense of abandonment by God, ends with the less-than-hopeful statement: 'Darkness is my only companion' (CEV). This feels hopeless, but it is vital to remember that the psalmist is talking to God. His words are a prayer. He is not having a crisis of faith. He is having a crisis of *connection*. He hasn't done anything wrong; he is not being punished; he just cannot find the connection with God that gave his life such energy in previous times. Similarly, Jesus' cry from the cross was not indicative of a crisis of faith. For the first time, he was experiencing a deep sense of disconnection. We can safely assume that Jesus loved God the Father, prayed enough and didn't have a lack of faith. Yet in his time of crisis, his cry was not answered; he experienced disconnection.

We can now see the importance of this in relation to how we might avoid disabling theologies when we are with people living with depression. There is a spirituality of darkness and disconnection within our tradition that we should recognize and reclaim. It is there in the psalms of lament. It is there in the words of Isaiah, and it is there in the words of Jesus. There is no shame in feeling disconnected from God as one encounters the storms of depression. Jesus has been there and continues to be there, waiting gently in the darkness for the time when we can reconnect and move back towards shalom. A mental health hermeneutic allows us to escape from disabling theologies that damage people and prevent them from experiencing the joy that is life with Jesus in good times and bad.

Enabling church

In concluding our discussion on mental health challenges and disability, we must return to the community of the local church and begin to think through some of the ways in which it can be a place of enablement that pushes against the disabling tendencies of both society and the Church. At the heart of Christian life is the practice of worship and community. We gather together as the body of Christ in order to worship God. The apostle Paul is quite clear that the thing which marks out the body of Christ is *diversity*. It is by finding unity in diversity that the beauty of humanity is revealed, and the inclusive nature of God's all-embracing love is revealed. It is therefore important that our worship practices do not become a source of disablement. They need to take full cognizance of the whole people of God. This is particularly important for those living with mental health challenges. There is not enough space here to develop this theme as fully as it deserves, but in closing we will highlight two possibilities for mentally healthy inclusive worship.

First, we need to think seriously about the kind of mental health hermeneutic that we have begun to develop in this chapter: a way of interpreting Scripture that takes seriously the limitations of human communication and the experience of mental health challenges. We have already seen the difficulties that can emerge if we read Scripture carelessly in relation to mental health. In 2 Timothy 3.16, we are told that: 'All scripture is inspired by God and is useful for teaching, for reproof, for correction, and for training in righteousness.' The God who is love (1 John 4.8) breathes out Scripture in order that we can live in his image. The intention of Scripture is to make us righteous. To be righteous is to be in right relationship with God. To be in right relationship with God is to love and be loved. The primary intention of Scripture, then, is to enhance our love for God, one another and ourselves (Mark 12.30–31). If that is the case, we must strive to ensure that this is how Scripture functions. This means we have to develop a hermeneutic that addresses the circumstances of people seeking a right relationship with God amid their mental health challenges. This does not mean that we have to change the meaning of the text to suit the nature of the congregation. All texts tend to be heard differently by people in different situations and circumstances. The point is that we need to be sensitive to meanings that may be hidden from us due to the limitations of our knowledge, communicational skills, or experience.

For example, in Philippians 4.6–7 (NIV) Paul says:

Do not be anxious about anything, but in every situation, by prayer and petition, with thanksgiving, present your requests to God. And the peace of God, which transcends all understanding, will guard your hearts and your minds in Christ Jesus.

A text like this will be heard quite differently by someone living with anxiety from the way it will be heard by others. The intention of the text is to assure us that God is in control and that it is God's peace that we seek after, even if our own peace is disturbed. However, an 'anxious reading' of such a scripture will assume that the experience of anxiety is a sign of condemnation, lack of faith, or some other spiritual concern. Such a reading adds to the struggles of anxiety rather than bringing peace. To preach such a text into the diversity of the body of Christ requires sensitivity, awareness and spiritual discernment.

I (John) visited a church not so long ago which had a preaching team. The team members gathered during the week to discuss the sermon for the following Sunday. The preacher preached the sermon to those in the group, and they gave feedback on style and content. They are considering including people with disabilities and people living with mental health challenges as part of that discernment group so that the impact of particular passages on particular groups of people can be brought to the fore. This is a good example of hermeneutical sensitivity. We want to emphasize again that the intention is not to change the meaning of the text, but to recognize the diversity of interpretations within a congregation and to minimize the chance of causing unnecessary suffering through unreflective interpretative assumptions. Not only does this avoid causing further harm to those who are already vulnerable by virtue of their mental health condition, but the rest of the congregation also gains in the process as they engage with different ways of thinking about the text, and the ministry of people with mental health challenges to the whole congregation is facilitated.

A second dimension of worship relates to the kinds of music that we play and sing. Music can be a real blessing, but it can also be very difficult for people. For example, if you are depressed and the congregation is constantly singing songs that indicate that you should be happy, times of worship can easily turn into an ordeal. I (Chris) met one Christian woman some years ago for whom this became such a struggle that she felt she couldn't go to church any longer. Here we are faced with the issue of liturgical discernment. If we take into consideration the diversity of the body of Christ as we put together our choice of music, it is wise to incorporate songs that sing of sadness and suffering. There are more psalms of lament within the Bible than any other form of psalm. We have seen that God has given us a language to articulate our sadness and brokenness. It is good that we should sing songs of glory. It is good that we should be happy as we worship. It is *not* good if our glorious happy songs are assumed to be marks of our faith or the only ways in which we can worship. We should not be forced to be ashamed of our brokenness. We need happy songs. We need sad songs. We need songs that reflect the body of Christ in all of its diversity.

Mental health challenges may or may not be disabilities, but, as we have seen, they are clearly a source of disablement within society and within the Church. If we are truly to come together as Christ's body, we need to take seriously what Paul says about the unity and diversity of that body (1 Corinthians 12). We are not all heads; we are not all feet; we are not all happy; we are not all well. But in all of our diversity and all of our different circumstances, we are one together. Ensuring that our worship and church life is not a source of disablement for some of our brothers and sisters is a key aspect of living faithfully with Jesus.

Conclusion

We have seen that the relationship between mental health challenges and disability is complex and controversial. Mental health conditions are disabling not solely (or even mainly) due to the impairments and activity restrictions that they often impose, but rather because of the negative interactions with social context and environment that produce participation restrictions. In many cases, the situation is made worse by discrimination and prejudice. This is a problem within wider society and in Christian churches, but churches also have disabling theologies which further complicate the situation. Disabling theologies enable us to manage our fears about mental health challenges in a seemingly Christian way, but in fact they do not stand up to closer examination. They are not biblical, and they further disable people facing mental health challenges. However, there is hope. A mental health hermeneutic which takes seriously the experiences of people living with mental illness, and which is inclusive of their insights and gifts, has the capacity to draw us all closer to God. Similarly, worship which is inclusive of sadness and lament, alongside joy and rejoicing, has the potential to enable us all to worship more honestly and deeply, participating as we do in both the Passion and the resurrection of Christ.

Biblical reflection

One day, while he was teaching, Pharisees and teachers of the law were sitting nearby (they had come from every village of Galilee and Judea and from Jerusalem); and the power of the Lord was with him to heal. Just then some men came, carrying a paralysed man on a bed. They were trying to bring him in and lay him before Jesus; but finding no way to bring him in because of the crowd, they went up on the roof and let him down with his bed through the tiles into the middle of the crowd in front of Jesus. When he saw their faith, he said, 'Friend, your sins are forgiven you.' Then the scribes and the Pharisees began to question, 'Who is this who is speaking blasphemies? Who can forgive sins but God alone?' When Jesus perceived their questionings, he answered them, 'Why do you raise such questions in your hearts? Which is easier, to say, "Your sins are forgiven you", or to say, "Stand up and walk"? But so that you may know that the Son of Man has authority on earth to forgive sins' – he said to the one who was paralysed – 'I say to you, stand up and take your bed and go to your home.' Immediately he stood up before them, took what he had been lying on, and went to his home, glorifying God. Amazement seized all of them, and they glorified God and were filled with awe, saying, 'We have seen strange things today.' (Luke 5.17–26)

This is a well-known story, often loved by Sunday schools. A story of solidarity, of a community refusing to let disability prevent one of its members from being able to encounter Jesus. In many ways, it is a beautiful and encouraging story. But maybe, sometimes, we miss out some of its deeper dynamics.

The 'paralysed man' is defined through nothing but his disability. He is given no name and is identified only through his impairment. What was he like, as a full person? Who was his family? What kind of friend was he? What skills did he have? What did he offer his community? Until Jesus speaks to him, he is passive, simply an object of other people's actions. Did he *want* to be brought to Jesus? What would he want from Jesus? How did he feel about being made the centre of attention?

It is easy to reduce people to one aspect of their being. It is easy to miss what they have to offer. What did it feel like to have the gaze of Jesus stop on him, and hear Jesus' words?

Jesus' words are very unexpected. Why say something about sin, rather than respond to what everyone else was thinking about?

Jesus does not see a 'paralysed man'. He sees a person, a full person, a moral agent, someone with choices, with a past, with regrets, with hopes. He sees a person just like every other person in the room. Much of Jesus' teaching had to do with transformation, with newness of life, with turning away from sin. In this one moment, Jesus places this man on a par with everyone else in the room. He gives him what every person watching also needs. Jesus models a way of relating in sharp contrast to that of the crowds pressing around him. He models seeing, listening, touching, responding to whole persons. And he calls every watcher and every reader to do the same.

Prayers

God of all people,
with all our differences and all our struggles,
may we learn to see ourselves and one another
as you see us:
frail and fragile, loved and cherished.
May we never put stumbling blocks
on the path of your children
through prejudice, fear or thoughtlessness.
Help us learn from one another,
that together we may learn
to live as your redeemed people,
sharing your life with those around us.
Amen

Loving and gracious God,
may this, my community, our community,
be a community of grace.
A place where mistakes are made and forgiven,
a place where mistakes are named and learnt from,
a place where we listen to intent underneath clumsy words,
and love sometimes hidden behind our frailties.
May I, may we, learn to be gracious in our speech,
hospitable in our lives
and forgiving in our relationships.
May our community
be one of welcome and grace,
where all can find their place
and all can grow to know you more deeply.
Amen

Questions to facilitate individual/group study

1 How do you respond to the idea of disability as, at least partly, a product of 'the interaction between a health condition and the social and physical environment'?
2 In what way might the physical, psychological, social or spiritual environment of your church enable or disable people?
3 What kind of responses have you given to others, or to yourself, in the face of mental health challenges in the past?
4 What kind of songs does your church/faith community sing? How far do songs and preaching reflect the whole gamut of human emotions?

Pointers to further reading

McCloughry, R. (2013), *The Enabled Life: Christianity in a disabling world*, London, SPCK.
World Health Organization and World Bank (2011), *World Report on Disability 2011.*

Chapter references

American Psychiatric Association (2013), *Diagnostic and Statistical Manual of Mental Disorders, Fifth Edition* (DSM-5), Washington, DC, American Psychiatric Association.

Cook, C. C. H. (2018), *Hearing Voices, Demonic and Divine: Scientific and theological perspectives*, London, Routledge.

Swinton, J. (2020), *Finding Jesus in the Storm: The spiritual lives of Christians with mental health challenges*, Grand Rapids, MI, Eerdmans.

6

Mental health and the mission of the Church

The word 'church' evokes many different thoughts, feelings and images. It may make us think of old, draughty buildings with uncomfortable wooden pews. It might be a warm, welcoming community. It may make us think of a bunch of random people singing together and listening to a sermon. Some might picture a warehouse with a band, flashy lights and contemporary worship. Others might picture tea and biscuits in a hall, grubby children spreading glitter in a church room, choirs rehearsing and maybe a minister talking quietly to a parishioner. In all of these, for church to be church, there will be people. People of many shapes and sizes, of different ages and with different lives; people who spend the majority of their lives *not* together, worshipping or having tea after a service, but engaged in all kinds of activities, jobs and relationships. And among all these people there will be some who are struggling in many ways, including with their mental health. And if we think of church gathered together, whether on Sunday or midweek, there will also be some people who are not there. Some will be absent for many reasons, including because life is just too hard, or church is just too difficult.

Some will be absent, too, not because they don't want to be there but because, as they wonder whether faith has anything to offer them, they are simply not sure about God, and not sure whether church would be a hospitable or generous place.

If we go back once again to the ministry of Jesus, and his widespread, open invitation to all people to come and see, come and follow, we might ask: how does church fit into this? How does church enable all those who are there, and not there, to know that the welcome of Jesus is on offer? And, more specifically for our purposes, how do churches nurture their life together so that those with mental health challenges can know that they are part of the community of faith, accepted and cherished, and in a place where their own faith, including their struggles, is part of the bigger picture, and contributes to the life and health of the whole?

'Mission', in this context, asks how the people of God share the love of God, both in their life together and in all their interactions – at home, at work, at play – and join in with what God is already doing in the world. Mission does not separate 'life together' from activities outside the Church, but rather takes the whole of what it means to be the people of God and explores what their vocation is. This will have outworkings in every area of life, and every area of life contributes to the Church's understanding of itself, of God, of human beings and of the world. Mission is not about defining an 'us' and a 'them' – this would risk falling into the kind of truncated relationships that lead people to caricature one another and not 'see' the full person. To think about mental health and the mission of the Church therefore is not to ask what the Church can do *for/to* those who struggle with mental health. It is not about separating people into groups of those who give and those who receive, those who are in need and those who are strong. Rather, it is about asking: what does it mean to be church together, to explore faith together and to share the love of God with those beyond the Church – whoever they are and whatever their circumstances? Mission therefore is something that all Christian people engage in, whoever they are and whatever their personal circumstances, in seeking to live as followers of Jesus Christ.

Various chapters in this book have touched on barriers to mission, ways in which the Church might have failed to be a generous and hospitable place for those with mental health struggles, or simply not known how to be hospitable, or not noticed that it wasn't. When churches perpetuate stigma or make it more difficult for those who struggle to hear of, receive and share the love of God, they fail in their vocation to be the people of God. The question is: what kind of practices, habits and beliefs can help churches fulfil their vocation more deeply?

Being church: exploring vocation

Earlier chapters have started to unearth possible answers to the question of how churches can better fulfil their vocation to be the people of God.

The chapter on stigma, for instance, reflected on expectations and what we imagine to be the 'ideal'. If we go back to the story of Job for a moment, we can see the crucial part that communities of faith play in shaping the experience of those who struggle. As we saw before, part of the problem that Job encountered was the belief system of his community, the idea that to have a good life (wealth, family, health) was to be blessed by God, and that to struggle meant being punished for wrongdoing. These underlying beliefs added to Job's distress. When his friends came to be with him, the same beliefs prevented them from responding well and making a generous and hospitable space for Job to process trauma and distress.

The importance of a worshipping community

The role of the community in Job is crucial, and not all negative. At the outset of Job's story, when the first disaster strikes, Job resorts to well-known practices and words:

> Then Job arose, tore his robe, shaved his head, and fell on the ground and worshipped. He said, 'Naked I came from my mother's womb, and naked shall I return there; the LORD gave, and the LORD has taken away; blessed be the name of the LORD.'
> (Job 1.20–21)

What Job does is resort to symbolic actions, or rituals, that others would have understood; he does not have to come up with new words or new theology, or find spontaneous ways of explaining how he feels. Instead, he uses words and actions that people throughout his whole community understand, and which connect him to their life together. Having set words and actions – prayers, liturgies, songs, rituals – can be crucial in enabling connection with God and the people of God in times of struggle, or when it is not even possible to make a logical or cognitive connection.

As a vicar, I (Isabelle) often went into nursing homes to lead acts of worship, including communion, and, at times, to pray with those who were coming to the end of their lives. I will always remember the first time I went into a home which cared for patients with severe dementia, when I was a trainee minister. As we gathered, people's attention was scattered; many talked to themselves or stared into space. There didn't seem to be much interest or focus as we read a short passage from Scripture, and I even wondered whether it was worth doing. But as we started a simple form of communion, using words and actions that most of those gathered knew, more and more people around the room were drawn in. When we said the Lord's Prayer, I could hear the words muttered all around the room, and see many eyes drawn towards me. It is one of the most holy moments I have ever experienced, as these folks were gathered by well-known words that connected them into life, church and community. At this moment, we were the people of God, worshipping together. It is worth stopping and wondering how our worship, week by week, and our practices day to day, might develop this kind of 'muscle memory' of prayer and connection, the kind of deep memory that can kick in when other parts of our selves might seem distant or damaged.

Going back to Job, symbolic words and actions are what Job reached for as his immediate reaction; unfortunately, these were not enough to sustain him beyond the first wave of catastrophe. Somehow, the words and concepts were not spacious enough, not broad enough to encompass where he was. This is where we come back to expectations and what our day-to-day worship and practices communicate. For our churches to be hospitable in times of struggle, the words, concepts and actions that we use need to be capacious and varied, but also attentive to underlying theologies. If a local congregation, for instance, mostly uses hymns and songs of praise and adoration, but forgets to include lament, it will skew the ability of all members of the congregation to participate. More worry-ingly, it will also create an expectation that Christian life should always be joyful, or that positive feelings towards God are the only ones acceptable. The shape and content of worship says something about what we think being church means and is for – it says something about vocation.

Most of the people who belong to local churches, if asked, will say that they want their church to be hospitable and welcoming; many will also say that they see their mission as reaching out in many different ways, including to those who struggle with their mental health. However, there can be a disconnect between this desire and the things that are commu-nicated through worship and the organization of life together. For a church to live out this vocation, its members have to build good, holy habits, interrogate their theology and explore how this kind of life can be lived to the best of their ability – and no church is ever perfect! Actually, building in an awareness of fallibility, a space for failure and grace, is part of shaping a community for true hospitality.

Truth and hope

To think of vocation is not to talk about impossible ideals; rather, it is to think about how we learn to live well in the world as it is, without being limited by the world as it is, but praying, 'Your kingdom come on earth as it is in heaven.' Shaping Christian communities is poised between radical truth and radical hope: it demands honesty about who we are, our failings and our limitations, and yet this reality can be transformed by hope and the knowledge that somehow God is at work among us and can do more than we think is possible. In the context of mission and mental health, to start with reality means to start with an understanding of the high incidence of mental health struggles, and the truth that our communities often tend to hide and stigmatize these.

I (Isabelle) once sat with a group of church leaders talking about mental health. A few of them banded together and claimed, 'But we don't really need any training or awareness raising, because there is no one in our congregations with any diagnosed mental illness.' Now, I had two comments in response. The first was: 'This is very unlikely. They simply haven't told you.' Research tells us that in groups of several hundred people, there inevitably will be quite a few people with a mental illness of some kind or another. Statistics suggest that worldwide, one in five adults is struggling with a common mental health disorder, and between 1 and 7 per cent with a major mental health disorder (Steel et al., 2014; Kessler et al., 2009). My second comment began with a question: 'Given what we know about the incidence of mental health struggles, *why* haven't your people told you? Or if you are right and there is no one in your congregation with a diagnosed mental illness, why on earth not? Given how prevalent mental health struggles are, there should be people in your congregations, and people your church members know, love, work with, live with, who do struggle this way.' In working together in our area, we needed to start with truth and reality – and repent of the things we had either done, or failed to do, that had led to churches being so disengaged with the reality of so many people's lives. The other part of naming truth and reality was much more hopeful; it was to acknowledge that in all likelihood there was kindness and hospitality happening, under the radar, for those who struggled with their mental health.

Church and mission are not just the 'official', 'organized' or 'visible' part of a church – they happen day to day, in the life of its members. By making these lives more visible, acknowledged and valued, the community could start to learn from what was done well, to listen to experiences that had previously been hidden, and to build something better together, exploring new meanings of the church's vocation.

Exploring mission and vocation, therefore, starts at home. It doesn't start with putting together a great 'programme' for those 'out there'; it starts with 'seeing' the patterns of life of local communities, with identifying all that is good and also what might hinder. It starts with seeing who is there, who is not there, and listening to stories. It starts with learning to be fully human, together.

Two stories

The question that follows 'Where do we start?' is, inevitably, 'What are we aiming for?' There is no 'one size fits all' answer. At one level, every congregation should have a 'minimum' standard, an expectation to be a good place, a 'real' place, where real people can share life as it is and struggle with God together rather than alone. But some will want to go further, to do something more specific. Before we look at some general principles for both, let's hear two stories of people and communities and how they embarked on this journey.

Ruth Rice and the Renew story

This is a story that Ruth shares in her own words:

> It's a surprising thing when the worst year of your life turns out to be the most fruitful.
>
> Several years ago, as a Christian leader, teacher, mum, wife and busy activist, I found myself unable to get out of bed – voice loss, depression, burnout for the worst part of a year. I had to relearn how

to pray, how to be . . . It was not until I felt I had no wellbeing that I began to be fascinated by what it actually is . . . this shalom that is deeper than our feelings and circumstances. I discovered rhythms of prayer and life in those dark days . . . meditation on psalms, simple prayers to punctuate the day, hobbies I had forgotten about. I couldn't think or reason myself out of it – I had to live through it. But I got so very isolated, found church too hard a place to be, and dreamt of a space where anyone could show up, bring a hobby, have a cuppa, pray if they wanted to, but together, not alone.

So as I crawled out of the year, together with the church I was leading, New Life Baptist Church in Nottingham, we set up Renew 37: a café-style space where all are welcome by name, not label, where all attend to wellbeing. There is a room with hobbies and activities suggested by all who attend and a quiet room attached where you can just be still and quiet, yet with company nearby. At intervals across the session we pause and invite anyone to join us as we pray our rhythms of prayer: a psalm, the Lord's Prayer, examen (rewinding the day). No pressure, just an invitation to share in learning about what wellbeing looks like.

Mental health professionals love what we are doing, its simplicity and boundaries.

Other churches began to visit and asked if we would help them set up a space, so we developed Renew Wellbeing as a charity with free online training and a relational ethos.

There are three simple principles:

- Be present: show up when you say you are going to show up; any faith and none, no trying to convert people.
- Be prayerful: spend time in the quiet space, be still, join in rhythms of prayer across the session.
- Be in partnership: develop relationships with mental health teams in the area so that the church can stick to simplicity and not try to fix people.

One lady told me she loved coming to Renew as now someone knew her name. She described her long lonely days before Renew existed where she could spend all week alone and the only way to hear her name spoken was to go to the GP. And this was before the self-isolation of a global pandemic.

This is a basic yet growing movement of presence, prayer and partnership. But it works for both church and community. There are now over 160 spaces nationwide, some ecumenical, some just one morning a week, some in church buildings, others in allotments or coffee houses . . . all becoming communities of wellbeing where it's OK not to be OK, where just showing up and being honest about wellbeing is bringing hope and peace.

Darren Howie

The second story is that of Darren Howie. Darren is the founder of a social enterprise, Sacred Bean, a coffee community pioneered and run by people overcoming life-controlling issues. Darren is also an ordained Church of England priest and a pioneer minister. But life started a long way from his new vocation. He grew up in a deprived, disadvantaged neighbourhood, in a broken home, and early on slid into a life of addiction and crime, gradually progressing from solvents to harder drugs. His mental health, already fragile through early adverse childhood experiences and trauma, spiralled down, and his life consisted of crime, heroin addiction and the revolving door of prison. There was little hope, and little help, as Darren was left to deal with the combined pain and trauma of what had been done to him and what he had chosen to do. A moment of breakthrough came, as Darren explains:

During my last ever prison sentence, ironically for a crime I didn't commit (a first for me), a prison chaplain came into my cell and told me I was going to die if I didn't accept help soon. It was a kind of epiphany moment (and I've needed many more since), where the veil between heaven and the hells of this earth became paper-thin. He spoke life to me: 'It doesn't have to be like this, you're better than your choices, your behaviour is not who you are, you are loved, you are important, and you are unique.' The God that he represented, the Christian God who is fully revealed in and through Jesus Christ, a

God who enters right into the heart of our human misery and mess, had a message for me: I was of supreme worth.

Darren's account of his relationship with the prison chaplain was one where he finally felt seen, as a full person. Not reduced to a 'drug addict' or a 'hopeless case' or a 'criminal', but a human being of immense worth. This first, initial encounter was only the start of a journey.

Discovering that he could be fully seen, and was worth loving, awakened hope in Darren, and a longing for something better, but this came with fear of what a different life would mean:

A new chapter in my story had begun, the journey had started, but I had a long way to travel. My family had disowned me. My son, who was only eight around this time, had found me six weeks previously with a belt round my neck trying to hang myself. I'd been in utter despair. I was ashamed of the person I'd become to feed my addiction. I was a six-and-a-half-stone heroin addict with no friends and a family who didn't want to know me. On leaving prison, based on new evidence that emerged to prove my innocence, the only clothes I possessed were the prison-issue ones I stood in. How was I ever going to wade through the physical, emotional and psychological debris of the tsunami that was my life? How would I navigate the practical implications and hurdles left in its wake? Even though I didn't have to accept the life I was living, or dread the changes needed to navigate the journey, I'd be lying if I said I wasn't terrified and overwhelmed by the mammoth task.

The next steps of Darren's story are shaped by the possibilities offered by communities of the people of God:

On my release, the chaplain got me into a 12-month, faith-based, residential rehabilitation community, where I would encounter more of this God in the community of his people and find a home I could call my own. Deep down this is what I longed for, though I never knew it back then: a loving family, a welcome embrace, a place to belong, a place to contribute: community.

It was there that I began to challenge and reject the labels that society had placed on me, such as 'once a smackhead, always a smackhead'. It was in this place that I had the first glimpse of my true worth, my true self, of the innocent little boy who'd been bruised by the big bad world and forced to survive. In the first church I was a member of after rehab, I went on to develop a faith in others, too, especially those who were different from me. They were life-givers and people who were there for me when I needed them the most. People who weren't put off by the messiness of ministering among reforming drug addicts or ex-offenders, or fazed by the regular relapses in the early days of my recovery. They were people who had the gift of grace and mercy in abundance, which slowly won me over and enabled me to find out who I was in the community of the other.

God in isolation did not offer or provide enough power or tools to keep me from stumbling on the journey. I needed people. All sorts of people. It was impossible to do it alone. I needed compassion, kindness and grace, most of which the systems and authorities lacked. This is why faith-based rehabs like the one I was in, and the diverse Christian community I belonged to afterwards, are vital for those in recovery. They create safe spaces for trust to grow and grace to be practised. Churches need to take risks with people like me. The gospel demands it of us.

I was transformed by being a part of a radical community of belonging. The people of my local church community, who welcomed me into their lives – and not just for two hours on a Sunday – were also transformed in the process. Here's the beautiful thing: the 'us and them' categories that plagued our respective subcultures began to slowly disintegrate. Peter was no longer just Peter the copper, our local bobby; he was Peter my friend who I played football with every week. Arthur was no longer just Arthur the headmaster of the local high school; he was Arthur my mentor and spiritual dad. The 'addict' and 'criminal' will only ever be fully transformed when the society in which they live is willing and committed to being trans-formed in the process. The problems of crime and addiction, and the trauma and disconnection they're rooted in, are not merely the problems or responsibilities of the 'addict' or the 'criminal' to 'fix', but our problems and responsibilities because we're all 'criminals' and 'addicts' in one way or another affected by trauma and disconnection. A lot can change when people are given the right context and culture from which to flourish. People like me can become a part of the solution to the world's problems and not just the cause.

Ruth and Darren's stories are unique; they are not a template or a model to imitate. But they can give us glimpses of hope, and glimpses of what kinds of thoughts, beliefs and practices can be taken up by churches eager to explore their vocation to generous and hospitable living in relation to mental health, and it is towards these glimpses and principles that we now turn.

Theology and underlying messages

Much of this book has explored how the ways in which we talk about God and the world – that is, our theology – shape our communities and our ability to live well together. Drawing these threads together and reflecting our two stories, first, our theology, at its most simple, has got to be one that enables us to meet every person as made in the image of God, and to accept his or her presence as a gift; and second, the things we say and do have to communicate the message that it is OK not to be OK.

In order to do this, churches have to draw on the whole of Scripture, and the whole of the Church's tradition of worship and prayer, in a way that makes space for suffering and illness as a normal part of human existence. To do this means that we can shape a language in churches to talk about the reality of mental health challenges, a language that is not defined solely by the world of mental health treatment and support, but is equally shaped by the reality that God is a God who walks with us through times of struggle. The language of mental health challenges needs to become part of the language of faith, another part of the experience and life that we bring before God and that God comes and dwells within.

This language is there already in the very Scriptures that we read: the Psalms, the prophets (especially Jeremiah) and the stories of those who struggle in many different ways in Scripture. Using stories is particularly powerful, though we need to allow the stories to speak for themselves, and not repackage them through easy hindsight. So, for instance, the prophet Jeremiah laments and mourns the loss of Jerusalem. His grief and trauma pour out onto the page. We know, reading Scripture, that Israel will come back from exile, that God still loves his traumatized and hurting people. But the fact is that this was not obvious to Jeremiah at the time when his words were spoken.

Later events cannot be used to diminish or qualify Jeremiah's distress. Or, to use a completely different image, when we read the story of the Passion of Jesus, we cannot just read it and think: it's all OK because he will rise from the dead. Somehow, we have to read the story of the Passion on its own terms, with its horror and uncertainty, and take seriously the fact that the risen Jesus still bears the scars of the crucifixion. The resurrection does not erase the cross, but it has the power to transform it.

One of the challenges for Christians today is to listen carefully to Scripture and listen carefully to the insights that mental health sciences bring and allow these two worlds occasionally to speak with the same voice, and often to speak with complementary voices, each shedding some light on the other, and broadening the vocabulary of our communities of faith to express and respond to mental health challenges.

Another aspect of theology that needs to be attended to is teaching on what it means to live well, what it means to live 'abundant life', in the words of the Gospel of John. There are two dangers here. One is that we speak of life uniquely shaped by the resurrection but forget the cross. The danger here is that we speak only of transformation, of hope, of new life, of healing, of joy. To speak of the Christian life is not to speak of an ideal life without suffering; rather, it is to speak of life where we can walk with God and one another even in the midst of suffering, where we can make good choices, and contribute to the common good in multiple ways even when life is hard and we face many different pressures and limitations. There is an equal and opposite danger to speaking of resurrection without the cross, however, and that is to focus so much on the cross that we forget the hope of resurrection.

The reality of suffering and challenges matters; it is true that often we only see God dimly, and struggle with our vocation and life in the world.

But just because we see dimly does not mean God is not there, or not at work. The Christian life is one that is lived on two planes: the reality of the world as it is, now, in its brokenness, and also the knowledge that Christ has come and brought change and transformation, that the God who came in Christ still walks with us every day and promises the renewal of all things. Somehow, our theology, our worship, our words and beliefs, have to capture this tension between cross and resurrection. They have to enable us to hold pain and hope closely together.

When it comes to pictures of 'the good life', we have to consider what message we give about what spirituality is *for*. Sometimes, churches run the risk of presenting life with God as some sort of self-help manual, or a path to happiness or self-actualization. If we do this, then to struggle with God and with mental health can easily be seen as a failure. But neither Scripture nor Christian tradition actually supports this caricature of the spiritual life. Rather, they both draw on the idea of a journey, a constant walk with God, a time of exploration and discovery; the journey is rarely easy, and contains challenges and obstacles, and sometimes wrong turns. But what matters is that it is a journey with God, and with one another, and on the journey we discover more of God, more of ourselves and more of one another. To use Eugene Peterson's phrase (taken from Nietzsche), discipleship is 'a long obedience in the same direction' (Peterson, 2000). The good life is defined primarily not by its end point or ideal quality, but by its walk, its direction, its determination to be open to God regardless of circumstances – even when this determination is dogged, half-reluctant or deeply unsure. It is a life defined by walking in the world as it is, with its challenges, pain and conflict – and with the God who promises to walk with us every step of the way.

Ordinary love

The two stories told above explore some of the basics of hospitality for those with mental health challenges. In Darren's case it is a story of normal, routine church, of how a local community of faith can be hospitable to all. In the case of Renew Wellbeing it is a story of a more intentional focus on mental health. Both, however, have something to say about the simplicity and power of ordinary, small acts of love.

Making space

The foundation of Renew Wellbeing is a story of awakening to the need to speak about God and form community differently. Renew Wellbeing stands out for its utter simplicity of vision; it is not a vision for great programmes of mission, with complex outreach, strategy and planning. If anything, it is a vision for doing *less* rather than more. And by doing less, space is made both for God to work in new ways and for people to meet one another and begin to relate as full human beings. As in Darren's story, power lies in the simplicity of what is done: meeting people where they are, loving them, sharing time, sharing bread and sharing life.

In both stories, people are seen as full human beings rather than being subsumed under a label – whatever the label is. For Darren it meant that he was seen for the first time as someone with potential, as a child of God, rather than an addict or criminal. In turn, he was able to see others as full human beings too, rather than reducing them to a role they play in his life (teacher, police officer, etc.). In both stories, hope emerges from building thicker, fuller relationships. As a general principle, it also means that in terms of mission, there is a need to create space for full relationships, to get to know people, and understand their *experience* of mental health challenges rather than just the category 'mental illness' or a diagnosis.

Meeting people where they are

The space created by Renew is also hospitable because it respects where people are 'at', does not push them to say or share more than they want, and involves the whole person rather than just words and concepts. Respecting where someone is at, and not trying to either fix or convert anybody, may seem to be a principle slightly at odds with 'mission'. In some ways, mission in general and evangelism in particular are specifically aimed at inviting people towards change, towards wholeness, and this often involves words, and, at times, in the life of the Church, has involved a great deal of attempts at persuasion. In the Renew Wellbeing example, we see the possibilities that are opened by the combination of a deeply distinctive Christian ethic (there is prayer, a rhythm of life; the space is explicitly Christian) and a simple trust that God can be at work without the need to try to actively 'convert' someone. This is another side of meeting and seeing the full person before us: whoever comes in is not seen as Christian/not Christian, healthy/ill, as an object of mission. He or she is simply another person who comes in and shares the life of the community. There is an invitation to share in prayer, but no expectation, and no second-guessing about what might lie behind the different ways in which people engage. In many ways, these spaces are dependent on a radical trust in God's presence, which can free members from the need to impose themselves, their views, their spirituality and expectations onto others.

Darren's story is somewhat different on the surface: he was drawn into a Christian community through a prison chaplain's concerned challenge to him; a major step after this was to engage with professional help through a therapeutic community. The local church did not try to offer the kind of help that belongs to specialists. Instead, its members engaged with him primarily by drawing him into the normal ebb and flow of their community life and extending ordinary love to him. It was the small things – the invitations for meals, the games of football – that spoke to him. Loving him as a full person opened up new possibilities for his transformation – and the transformation of the local church alongside. The church offered Darren something very different and distinctive: people to walk alongside him, textured relationships, and life together. In his story, professional help and the love of the Christian community walked hand in hand.

Boundaries and collaborative working

These two stories highlight the need for churches to be clear about the boundaries of what they can and cannot do, and therefore to work collaboratively with others. To think about mission and mental health does not mean replacing statutory services or offering an alternative. It means doing what the church can do best, while understanding what others need to do, without interference. A good place to start for the leaders of any church considering how mental health questions fit into its life and mission would be to increase people's own understanding of mental health challenges; there are courses and basic training available for church members, which can be accessed easily and help to lay foundations for a better life together (see Appendix A). Part of any initial training will involve mapping out what partners there may be in this work, when it is appropriate to seek help, and setting appropriate boundaries for involvement.

Boundaries can be a difficult concept in churches. The greatest strength of being a church is that we deal with the whole of life. We do not just offer a specialist, professional space, but a space for every aspect of life. That is immensely powerful, as we saw with Darren. But this strength can also lead into difficult areas, because edges are blurred; it is easy to simply want to 'help' but not know how, or try to help in ways that are actually either unsustainable or unhelpful. People with mental health challenges may have to face helpers who, like Job's friends, are keen to 'fix' or help, and get either over-involved or involved in unhelpful ways. Therefore it is important to be able to have conversations about what it means to be hospitable, to open one's home or to share lives, and what the boundaries to each of these might be. To be hospitable does not mean to have no boundaries; rather, it means to hold boundaries generously, kindly, and with the willingness to learn and change.

To have boundaries means to know who I am, what I need, what I can do, and what I am not able to give, or do, or be. Being honest about these, as individuals and as communities, can help create a safer space for all, with clear expectations and an acknowledgement of our limitations – even when these limitations may be painful because we want to give, or receive, more than what is possible.

Churches have to be clear about what their role can be – they can offer community spaces, places of welcome and acceptance, additional support and general pastoral care, and they can fight stigma. When appropriate training is on offer, it is possible to build additional provision such as advocacy or mental health first aid. Care happens at multiple levels – from the day-to-day, normal relationships between people, to more intentional forms of care, through, for instance, pastoral care teams, wellbeing champions and the pastoral role of leaders. Those with more specific and intentional responsibilities need to work within a framework of clear boundaries and accountability. Their work needs to be done sensitively, and within the right context, so that safeguarding protocols are observed, and volunteers as well as paid staff are clear about when and how to refer someone for further help. Church leaders have a specific role here in helping congregations to be self-aware and intentional about the kind of help they may be offering, about boundaries and about accountability.

Nurturing communities of grace

The need for collaboration and an understanding of appropriate boundaries and limitations takes us back to an earlier theme, that of realism and self-awareness. Different churches will have something different to offer, and different challenges in offering it. In addition, no church, no community, will ever be perfect in its efforts to be hospitable, inclusive and fully loving, sometimes because of simple failure, sometimes because it is just not possible to give others the level of care or help needed. The starting point of Christian spirituality is an awareness of our frailty as human beings and our propensity to get things wrong. This is not meant to be paralysing, or frightening, but liberating. It is about working with who we are, rather than idealized versions of who we should be. We do not need to wait for perfection to do something; nor is failure ever final. Christian spirituality is first and foremost a spirituality of grace.

Grace is at the heart of the gospel – not the kind of cheap grace that says that bad things and actions do not matter, but the kind of grace that enables us to recognize that all human beings and human systems fail in many ways, and to commit ourselves to forgiveness and learning from mistakes. No community can be hospitable without grace. Without grace, mistakes are held against people; there is no space for forgiveness or doing better next time. A community without grace is one where people are written off for their mistakes, and those who either fail or are failed by others walk away. A community of grace seeks to find ways of walking together even when we hurt one another, do not understand one another, fail in the things we do and the things we fail to do, as Anglicans say in their liturgy of penitence.

Grace works in several ways as we think about mission and mental health. It needs to be practised in a community so that it becomes part of the furniture, as it were. Grace can free a local community to take new steps and try new things; being steeped in grace also means an open attitude towards the other, towards difference, and less focus on what 'should' happen. It has the potential to open up a more hospitable, freer space for others to enter. Grace also means that if someone new, a visitor, does something that may be thought of as a little strange, or different, this can be accepted in ways that allow difference to be loved rather than rejected.

A church I (Isabelle) visited recently has a strong ministry within the city centre where it is located. As a city church, it is a warm, hospitable place for many people who are homeless and struggling with their mental health. During the Sunday service, someone walked in at the back and started shouting and swearing at the preacher. None of the regular members turned round to stare at the interruption; the person coming in was not treated as a spectacle or as an unwelcome interruption to the flow of the service. The vicar at the front just said, 'Oh hello, Sheila, it's good to see you', and carried on. Meanwhile, one of the churchwardens went to meet her and offered her a cup of tea and a sandwich. She actually is a regular visitor to the church, though does not engage in the way that most church members engage. But she has a place, and is accepted, and was not excluded or made to feel that she had broken the rules – though neither was she encouraged to keep interrupting. People in the church had taken time to get to know her, and knew who she was and what she needed, and simply responded to that and loved her as she was. By the end of the service, when everyone was milling about for coffee, she was sitting in a chair and chatting at the top of her voice.

Sitting light to rules and expectations of 'what we do' is a key feature of this church's ministry in its time and place. It is not, however, something that just 'happened'. It came with a conscious effort to be a hospitable place, some false starts, and many failures along the way as the church and its visitors tried to learn together how to live well together. Many of those who are homeless have complex challenges, including with their mental health. The church was keen to reach out and provide something different from what was already out there, and started a café with a hot meal, straight after the evening service, which gradually led to people coming in to the services more generally. There were some early setbacks as the church tried to 'reach out' in ways that were uninformed and slightly naive, with the result that, at the homeless café, violence erupted, and drugs were found on the premises. The leaders and congregation had to rethink what boundaries needed to be put in place so that all would be safe. Early on, the church also had an underlying drive to try to 'fix' people, to offer help, to enable people to step into a life that the Christians judged to be 'better'. As time went on, they learned that the people who visited needed to be listened to about their own needs, desires and goals. Working together took time, listening and negotiation, and growing partnership with other organizations. Over time, they learned to do what a church could do: be a community that loved and walked with others. No church is perfect, but churches can be good enough, and open to learning more.

Engaging with the big picture

So far this chapter has largely considered local questions, linked to relationships and communities. There is of course a bigger canvas on which to consider the mission of the Church. Mission can go beyond what we do in the local area, and get involved with the bigger, systemic issues linked to mental health. Those with mental health challenges often experience other challenges, either deriving from, or as triggers to, mental health struggles. Any group of people that experiences prejudice on account of their identity, or economic deprivation, or any other factor, will also experience higher levels of mental health challenges (Dinos, 2014). Therefore, an ethical question arises in terms of mission: if there is such overlap between deprivation and disadvantage, and mental health challenges, is it right to only try to respond at the level of meeting the individual? This is another version of Desmond Tutu's famous aphorism, 'There comes a point where we need to stop just pulling people out of the river. We need to go upstream and find out why they're falling in.' There is a complex relationship and bidirectional relationship between stigma and mental health problems. Different sources of stigma (e.g. race, sexuality, gender identity, offender status) may further contribute to this vicious circle. Poverty is also contributory to mental health problems, quite apart from stigma. To look at the whole person therefore means that we cannot isolate mental health as the only or main component of a person to be interested in. We need to hear someone's whole story and respond to the whole story.

The biblical tradition of lament takes us very firmly in this direction. In the individual psalms of lament, the person speaking expresses deeply personal, individual, heartfelt suffering, and cries out to God, often complaining and taking God to task for not acting or for seeming to be absent. The cry of lament is more than just a complaint or an expression of pain, however. It is also a cry for justice, for things to be put right. This is why so many laments contain, at some point, the question 'Why?' By addressing lament to God, the person praying, or the community praying, is not asking simply for personal redress or healing, but petitioning the King of the universe for systemic change, for a righting of wrongs, for the ushering in of a better, healthier community. Lament is an intensely political act, because it says, 'The way things are is not right; the course of life needs to change.' If, therefore, we argue for the reintroduction of the language of lament and pain in our churches, then we are inviting churches to go beyond the personal and individual and ask questions about *why* certain people are so disproportionately affected by mental health challenges, by poverty, by racism and so on.

Asking these questions is always dangerous, because it may take us to places where we can no longer stay silent and have to get involved. This is where churches that are serious about mission and mental health may find themselves looking beyond their own interactions and local projects and asking whether there is more they could do. The answer, of course, is that there *is* more that can be done. But the multiplicity of choices can, as always, be bewildering, and the Christians in each local community will have to prayerfully consider which areas of involvement are right for them at this point: it could be advocacy, partnership with charities, social action, political involvement and so on. There is no formula, other than perhaps the need to work humbly and in partnership again. There are many organizations already involved in this area, and, in choosing how to proceed, churches may want to ask the following questions:

- Where do we see God at work in existing projects and charities?
- What can our church/group do that supports and joins in with what is already happening?

- Are there gaps to be filled, something new to do?
- How can we work most effectively to see change in our communities and wider society?
- How does the local context shape and inform our engagement on a wider scale?

Practices, rituals and holy habits

Whether a church wants to do something special and focused, or simply think about its more general life and mission, or become involved beyond its locality in campaigning and wider social issues, the starting point is largely the same: it needs to start with good, simple, holy habits for individual Christians and in their life together. Building holy habits takes time, practice and intentionality. But it is worth it: holy habits can be the solid foundation, the rock on which to build a stronger house – to use an image from Jesus' parables. Holy habits, or virtues, feature frequently in the Bible. We see them extolled in the book of Proverbs, in the Psalms, in the teaching of Jesus such as the Sermon on the Mount and, most clearly, in the letters of the New Testament – in James, in Peter and in Paul's epistles. The kinds of attitudes that holy habits foster are celebrated in Paul's famous list of the fruits of the Spirit: 'the fruit of the Spirit is love, joy, peace, patience, kindness, generosity, faithfulness, gentleness, and self-control' (Galatians 5.22–23). These attitudes, or virtues, foster good community relationships and the kind of attentiveness to the other that we have talked about in this book. They are both a sign of the presence of God, and something we can nurture in life together as a response to God's presence. In many ways, the list is foundational for anything else we might do; as Paul says elsewhere, if we do not have love, we have nothing. If we think of the Church's mission in the context of mental health, but we do not have love or kindness or gentleness or generosity, then our efforts are likely to amount to nothing. It is precisely these things that can help us be communities of grace, of forgiveness, of genuine partnership and openness to the other.

The question, therefore, as we approach the end of this chapter, is to ask, beyond the general: what kind of habits can help churches be hospitable places for those who struggle with their mental health? In this chapter and throughout the book, we have alluded to and explored different threads, different ideas and practices that can help transform our life together, and help Christian communities become more hospitable and able to share the profound love of God for every person. Some of these are now gathered here as a possible list of practices to nurture consciously.

To see and hear better

- **Seeing the whole person**: not reducing someone to a diagnosis, or a problem, or a need for help, but making a conscious effort to get to know the whole person.
- **Building up knowledge and understanding**, not just of 'mental illness' in general (though this matters too) but of the *experience* of mental illness in those we meet.
- **Attending to absence**: who might not be present in our communities, and why? It is a holy habit to ask regularly whether someone has gone missing from among us, or whether there are people who are never there, and can never be there.
- **Attending to presence**: this is about seeing who is there, and how they are present, just as Jesus 'saw' the blind man and responded; noticing who is isolated, not speaking, or shunned.
- **Listening to the other's experience of God**: what can this different experience contribute to the spirituality and life of faith of the whole community?

To speak better

- **Paying attention to language**: how do we speak about mental health challenges? How do we speak about specific people? How do we speak about God? Regularly examining our language – the things we say in conversation, in prayer, in songs – can help us be alert to stigma and hidden expectations.
- **Broadening topics of worship, teaching and prayer** so that struggling with God is a normal part of the language and discussion of faith.
- **Valuing different spiritualities**: making space for different experiences of God to be brought into worship and sharing.

To do better

- **Practising 'ordinary love'**: being aware of small gestures and the power of ordinary things, such as chatting to a visitor, inviting someone round, sharing lives rather than just words.
- **Working 'with', rather than 'for'**: ensuring that we are working with people as people, as members of our community, who have agency and insight, in partnership.

These are good habits; they can help. Ultimately, however, just as the apostle Paul writes, be patient, be kind, be hopeful and, above all, love.

Conclusion

Every Christian congregation should have a 'minimum' standard, an expectation to be a good place, a 'real' place, where real people can share life as it is and struggle with God together rather than alone. Drawing on the language of the whole of Scripture, and the whole of the Church's tradition of worship and prayer, churches need to make space for suffering and illness as a normal part of human existence. Offering 'ordinary love', and welcoming people with mental health challenges as they are, we have an opportunity to participate in God's extraordinary love for those who struggle.

Biblical reflection

O LORD, you have searched me and known me.
You know when I sit down and when I rise up;
    you discern my thoughts from far away.
You search out my path and my lying down,
    and are acquainted with all my ways.
Even before a word is on my tongue,
    O LORD, you know it completely.
You hem me in, behind and before,
    and lay your hand upon me.
Such knowledge is too wonderful for me;
    it is so high that I cannot attain it.

Where can I go from your spirit?
    Or where can I flee from your presence?
If I ascend to heaven, you are there;
    if I make my bed in Sheol, you are there.
If I take the wings of the morning
    and settle at the farthest limits of the sea,
even there your hand shall lead me,
    and your right hand shall hold me fast.
If I say, 'Surely the darkness shall cover me,
    and the light around me become night',
even the darkness is not dark to you;
    the night is as bright as the day,
    for darkness is as light to you.
(Psalm 139.1–12)

Psalm 139 is a strange psalm. Different people read it differently. It can be a psalm of immense comfort – reassuring us of God's constant presence and care. Or it can be a psalm of fear and discomfort – with the worry of God's oppressive presence, or a stinging awareness of God's apparent absence despite the promise of presence.

Spend some time reading the words, pondering what they mean to you. Do you welcome God's presence in every area of your life? Are there places, or times, when this presence feels oppressive, or elusive or distant?

I often wonder about the psalmist's flight into darkness, wishing the light to recede and the darkness to cover him. Have you ever felt this? Do you know anyone else who has?

What might it look like to speak the words of this ambivalent psalm when we meet for worship or study as people of God? What might it look like to acknowledge the ambivalence of our faith, and the times when we struggle with God's presence, or God's seeming absence?

For it was you who formed my inward parts;
    you knit me together in my mother's womb.
I praise you, for I am fearfully and wonderfully made.
    Wonderful are your works;

that I know very well.
  My frame was not hidden from you,
when I was being made in secret,
  intricately woven in the depths of the earth.
Your eyes beheld my unformed substance.
In your book were written
  all the days that were formed for me,
  when none of them as yet existed.
(Psalm 139.13–16)

The psalm continues with a ringing affirmation that God has created every person and knows each one intimately. If every person is this precious to God, what does that mean about how we see ourselves? And what does it mean about how we regard, relate to and treat every other person?

How might we meet together, speak together, reach out together, in ways that enable others to see themselves as precious to God, especially when they profoundly doubt their own worth?

The psalmist gives us a little bit of a clue:

How weighty to me are your thoughts, O God!
  How vast is the sum of them!
I try to count them – they are more than the sand;
  I come to the end – I am still with you.
(Psalm 139.17–18)

There is something tentative in these lines, a recognition of our finitude over and against the vastness of God. An affirmation of God's immensity and care, and a recognition that we, as human beings, often struggle to understand.

How might this tentativeness help us shape our mission and ministry? How might it help us make spaces that are open to surprise, open to hearing different ways in which God is at work?

The psalm does not end there. It would be much easier if it did. But this is a psalm of light and shadows, a psalm of contradictions and ambivalence. It now moves into a passionate plea for justice:

O that you would kill the wicked, O God,
    and that the bloodthirsty would depart from me –
those who speak of you maliciously,
    and lift themselves up against you for evil!
Do I not hate those who hate you, O LORD?
    And do I not loathe those who rise up against you?
I hate them with perfect hatred;
    I count them my enemies.
Search me, O God, and know my heart;
    test me and know my thoughts.
See if there is any wicked way in me,
    and lead me in the way everlasting.
(Psalm 139.19–24)

Just like every human being, the psalmist is not a disembodied person, speaking in generalities about an ideal state. The psalmist is caught in forces beyond his own person, and those forces shape his desires, fears, hopes and ambivalent relationship to God. The cry of his heart, right at the end, reminds us to see the whole person and the forces that act upon him; it is true for ourselves, and for those we seek to welcome, support or embrace.

Yet with timeless wisdom, the psalmist ends with an invitation to God to test and lead him – an acceptance of his vulnerability and limitedness, a willingness to grow in self-awareness, and an embrace of the transformation that comes when we enter into relationship with the God who created us, and knows us intimately.

Prayers

Gracious and loving God,
help us in all our interaction
to be a hospitable people;
at home, at work, at worship, at play,
may we share lives
and be attentive to your presence in the lives of others.
Teach us to be truthful and vulnerable,
and hold together the fragility of our world

with the reality of your presence
and the hope of resurrection.
Amen

God of kindness and patience,
help me show your own kindness and patience to myself
and those around me when mental health struggles
change or overshadow the course of our lives.
In all things, may I make space to listen
to you, to myself and to others,
and be ready to see glimpses of your glory
in all places, even the most unexpected.
In Jesus' name,
Amen

Questions to facilitate individual/group study

1 Do you/your worshipping community ever speak of mental health in connection to mission? If so, how is this talked about?
2 What parts of the daily or weekly worship that you experience have the potential to help you connect with God and church at difficult times?
3 How do you respond to Ruth and Darren's stories? Is there anything that you could draw on and adapt in your own context?
4 What does 'abundant life' look like for you?
5 Out of the list of practices and holy habits, which do you already use? Which do you warm to most, and why? What might you want to try?
6 What does 'ordinary love' look like for you and your local community?
7 What can churches do that mental health services cannot do to facilitate recovery from mental illness?

Pointers to further reading

Cook, C. C. H. (2020), 'Mental Health and the Gospel: Boyle Lecture 2020', *Zygon* 55(4), pp. 1107–23.
—— (2020), 'Mental Health in the Kingdom of God', *Theology* 123(3), pp. 163–71.
Rice, R. (2021), *Slow Down, Show Up and Pray: Simple shared habits to renew wellbeing in our local communities*, Milton Keynes, Authentic.

Chapter references

Dinos, S. (2014), 'Stigma Creating Stigma: A Vicious Circle', *Psychiatric Bulletin* 38(4), pp. 145–7.

Kessler, R. C., S. Aguilar-Gaxiola, J. Alonso, S. Chatterji, S. Lee, J. Ormel, T. B. Üstün and P. S. Wang (2009), 'The Global Burden of Mental Disorders: An Update from the WHO World Mental Health (WMH) Surveys', *Epidemiology and Psychiatric Sciences* 18(1), pp. 23–33.

Peterson, E. A. (2000), *Long Obedience in the Same Direction: Discipleship in an instant society*, Westmont, IL, IVP.

Steel, Z., C. Marnane, C. Iranpour, T. Chey, J. W. Jackson, V. Patel and D. Silove (2014), 'The Global Prevalence of Common Mental Disorders: A Systematic Review and Meta-Analysis 1980–2013', *International Journal of Epidemiology* 43(2), pp. 476–93.

Conclusion

In this book we have explored some of the challenges that mental illness presents for Christians. Of course, the challenges of illness, trauma, stigma, prejudice, discrimination or disability can affect anyone, whether Christian or not. However, we have seen that there are ways in which Christian theology or spirituality can help to overcome such challenges, and there are ways in which they can make life more difficult. Disabling theologies, and theologies that reinforce stigma, need to be identified and rebutted. It is hard enough struggling with depression without being told that it is due to your lack of faith. The challenge of schizophrenia is only made worse by being told that it is due to demonic influence. The aim of the book has been partly to draw attention to some of these unhelpful ways of thinking and behaving, so as to avoid falling into traps that only make the experience of mental illness even more of a struggle than it needs to be.

There are, however, many positive ways in which Christian faith is helpful to those struggling with mental health challenges. Research shows that Christian belonging and believing are associated with better mental health and better outcomes.[13] Why might this be? We have explored a number of possible answers to this question in the earlier chapters of this book.

At its best, belonging to a Christian community offers a supportive network of relationships – with God and other people – that allows human beings to flourish. Loving, and being loved, affirms our identity as creatures made in God's image, and as followers of Jesus who are known for their love of one another. Mental wellbeing is fostered by

---

13 At least in comparison with most non-religious people. There is no current scientific evidence that Christians fare any better than members of other faith traditions – but much more research is needed. As discussed earlier in the book, there are some ways in which Christian faith might make mental health challenges more – rather than less – difficult to manage.

this acceptance and affirmation, and, when we do struggle, it makes the struggles seem more manageable. We share them with one another, rather than hiding them away as something to be ashamed of, so that those who struggle do not struggle alone. We recognize that Christian communities do not always live up to this high ideal, but it is central to the mission of the Church that it should seek out those who struggle and stand alongside them.

When mental health becomes mental ill health, and when we struggle with emotions, appetites, thoughts, voices, behaviours or relationships, Christian spirituality offers some really helpful resources for coping. Giving and receiving forgiveness, seeking God's support and comfort, working together with God, doing what we believe to be right, and finding positive ways of reimagining what God is doing in our lives, all help us to cope better. At the same time, mental images of our problems as God's way of punishing us, the devil's way of attacking us, or the things that other Christians have done to hurt us, all do not help, and we need to find ways of putting them to one side. We may need assistance in doing this, and spiritual direction, counselling or psychiatry can all play their part. Recovery colleges, and Christian groups such as FRIENDS (see Chapter 4) or Renew Wellbeing (see Chapter 6), can provide friendship and support in recovery and a place to learn from others going through similar experiences.

Mental health challenges can sometimes make it seem as though we are struggling to swim against God's tide. It feels as though God is a part of the problem, not the answer. Prayer is not a magic solution that takes away all our struggles. Like Paul, we may find that our prayers are not answered as we would like and that we face the challenge of experiencing God's power made perfect amid our weakness. Like Jesus on the cross, we may find ourselves asking why God has forsaken us. None of this is 'OK', but we need to be honest about such experiences. It is – in the language of Renew Wellbeing – 'OK not to be OK'. Prayer is the context within which Christians engage with all of this. It is sometimes a struggle, but – however it may appear – God is always alongside us in this struggle. That is categorically *not* a platitude to be rolled out every time we meet someone who does not feel OK. It is, rather, a truth prayerfully and patiently to be learned as we meet one another amid our sharing of mental health struggles, together following in the footsteps of Jesus and finding ourselves with him in Gethsemane or on Calvary.

As we explored in the final chapter of this book, the language of mental health challenges needs to become part of the language of faith. We have grown accustomed to talking about mental health with the language of healthcare, and about faith with the language of theology. We have separate conversations about mental health and about Christian faith. We do not find this separation of the conversations in Scripture. Mental illness, mental health challenges, are another part of the experience of life that we bring before God in prayer. They are experiences amid which God comes alongside us. They are all a part of the language of prayer. There clearly are boundaries between what can be offered in churches and what is provided within the health services. However, we can bridge these boundaries in important ways. We need to get better at seeing a daily dose of medication as a prayer for healing (where the act of taking medication becomes prayerful), and a prayer offered from a place of emotional darkness as an important psycho-spiritual therapy, all with the hope of finding that Jesus was alongside us in our struggles all the time.

In the Introduction, we considered briefly the story in Luke's Gospel of a woman afflicted with a spirit of weakness. At the beginning of the story the woman is emotionally and physically disabled. Her identity – for 18 years – has been that of a woman who struggles with spiritual, emotional and physical diminishment of identity. We might well have imagined that she needed Jesus to provide some deliverance ministry, to cast out the spirit that afflicted her, but Jesus does not respond to her needs in this way. Luke – the good physician – blurs the boundaries and presents this as a healing miracle, not as an exorcism. Jesus recognizes that she was, all along, a daughter of Abraham. In the eyes of others – perhaps in her own eyes – she may have appeared so much less than this, but, in the midst of her struggles, she was faithful, chosen and beloved. Jesus sets her free by healing her, but he also sets us free by enabling us to see her for who she really was all along.

A paradox of Christian life is – as St Paul explained to the Corinthian church – that God's power is made perfect in weakness (2 Corinthians 12.9). Things are therefore often not as they seem. A woman afflicted by a spirit of weakness may actually be a faithful daughter of Abraham.

A person struggling with mental illness may actually be flourishing in faith, hope and love. Christian resilience is revealed not in our ability to sail through life in good weather but in the faith that enables us to find Jesus amid the storm. It is about holding on in faith, but, perhaps more importantly, it is about discovering that Jesus is holding on to us. The spirituality of good mental health is thus not one of empty platitudes, attribution of demonic affliction, or spoiled identities. The Christian spirituality that is worth its name is to be found struggling with Jesus in Gethsemane and on Calvary, in the hope of sharing also in his resurrection. Our hope and our prayer is that the things we have presented in this book can help all of us to live into this vision.

Appendix A
Some useful resources

Christian charities offering information, training and resources

- **Mind and Soul Foundation** – a national charity that seeks *to educate*: sharing the best of Christian theology and scientific advances; *to equip*: helping people meet with God and recover from emotional distress; *to encourage*: engaging with the local church and mental health services: <www.mindandsoulfoundation.org>.
- **Renew Wellbeing** – a national Christian charity training and supporting churches to open simple, safe, sustainable places where 'it's OK not to be OK': <www.renewwellbeing.org.uk>. Read *Slow Down, Show Up and Pray* by Ruth Rice (Authentic Media, 2021), which tells the story of Renew Wellbeing and provides practical advice for setting up a Renew Wellbeing Centre in your church and locality.
- **Sanctuary** – the Sanctuary Course from Sanctuary UK: <www.sanctuarymentalhealth.org/uk>. The Sanctuary Course is a free online resource to facilitate mental health awareness and tackle stigma. Combining elements of psychology, theology and lived experience, Sanctuary offers a range of resources and training to support a whole-church approach to mental health and wellbeing.

Church of England resources

- *Supporting Good Mental Health* by Professor Chris Cook is a PDF booklet, also available as 13 audio reflections, which aims to support mental health: <www.churchofengland.org/resources/mental-health-resources/supporting-good-mental-health>.
- *Minority Ethnic Mental Health Toolkit* provides information on UK minority ethnic mental health: <www.churchofengland.org/resources/mental-health-resources/uk-minority-ethnic-mental-health-toolkit>.

- Liturgical resources are available from: <www.churchofengland .org/sites/default/files/2021-10/Liturgical%20Resources%20for %20Mental%20Health-Wellbeing.pdf>.

Interfaith resources

- **Mental Health Ministries** – a website that offers a wide variety of downloadable print and media resources, with a focus on faith and spirituality in recovery and treatment. It has some useful liturgical resources for Christian worship: <www.mentalhealthministries.net /resources/worship_resources.html>.

Secular agencies and resources

- **American Psychiatric Association Foundation** – publishes *Mental Health: A guide for faith leaders*, a useful guide to mental health for faith leaders which is authoritative and accessible. Resource links within the guide are for the USA, but the general information is invaluable and internationally relevant: <www.psychiatry.org/File%20Library /Psychiatrists/Cultural-Competency/Mental_Health_Guide_Tool_Kit _2018.pdf>.
- **Mental Health Foundation** – works to prevent mental health problems by means of community programmes, research, public engagement and advocacy. The website has a wealth of useful and reliable information: <www.mentalhealth.org.uk>.
- **Mind** – a national charity offering comprehensive information on all aspects of mental health: <www.mind.org.uk>.
- **Royal College of Psychiatrists** – the professional body responsible for training and standards in psychiatry in the UK. The mental health information section of its website offers useful resources for patients and carers: <www.rcpsych.ac.uk/mental-health>. In addition, the Spirituality & Psychiatry Special Interest Group of the College has a useful archive of papers: <www.rcpsych.ac.uk/members/special -interest-groups/spirituality/publications-archive>.
- **Mental Health First Aid Training** – provides workplace-based training to support good mental health: <https://mhfaengland.org>.

Getting help

- The NHS supplies a list of mental health charity helplines and also provides access to local NHS emergency helplines: <www.nhs.uk /mental-health/nhs-voluntary-charity-services/charity-and-voluntary -services/get-help-from-mental-health-helplines>.

Books

Coleman, M. (2016), *Bipolar Faith: A black woman's journey with depression and faith*, Minneapolis, MN, Fortress.

Cook, C. C. H. (ed.) (2013), *Spirituality, Theology and Mental Health*, London, SCM Press.

Cook, C. C. H., and I. Hamley (eds) (2020), *The Bible and Mental Health: Towards a biblical theology of mental health*, London, SCM Press.

Greene-McCreight, K. (2015), *Darkness Is My Only Companion: A Christian response to mental illness*, Grand Rapids, MI, Brazo Press.

Rice, R. (2021), *Slow Down, Show Up and Pray: Simple shared habits to renew wellbeing in our local communities*, Milton Keynes, Authentic.

Rose, S., et al. (2016), *Fifteen Steps Out of Darkness: The way of the cross for people on the journey of mental illness*, Maryknoll, NY, Orbis.

Swinton, J. (2020), *Finding Jesus in the Storm: The spiritual lives of Christians with mental health challenges*, Grand Rapids, MI, Eerdmans.

Webb, M. (2017), *Toward a Theology of Psychological Disorder*, Eugene, OR, Cascade.

Appendix B
Intercessions for mental health

Heavenly Father, hear us as we pray for ourselves, for one another, for your Church and for a needy world.

We pray for those who are anxious, isolated, lonely or grieving because of the Covid-19 pandemic. We pray for all those who are separated from the ones they love because of social distance, self-isolation or shielding. We pray for those whose mental health has suffered because of the impact of the pandemic on our lives, our jobs and our economy.

Lord, in your mercy,
hear our prayer.

We lament the stigma and prejudice that infected our attitudes to mental illness long before Covid-19 appeared. We pray for all who have not been made welcome in our churches, our communities, our homes or our hearts. We remember especially the homeless, prisoners, the poor, members of the UK's minority ethnic or LGBTQ communities, and all those whose mental health has suffered because of exclusion, prejudice, discrimination, rejection, bullying or cruel words.

Lord, in your mercy,
hear our prayer.

We pray for all whose thoughts or feelings are troubled. We pray for those who are depressed, anxious or afraid, for those who feel that you are far away from them, and for those who feel that life is not worth living. We pray for those whose high moods endanger their wellbeing and that of those around them. We pray for those who hear voices that are intrusive, threatening, abusive or evil. We pray for those whose thoughts are dominated by delusional beliefs. We pray for those who struggle with cravings for alcohol, drugs, food, gambling or sex. We pray for those who suffer from anorexia, and for all whose body image is a source of distress to them.

Lord, in your mercy,
hear our prayer.

We pray for relatives, friends, carers, and all who struggle with the impact of mental ill health on relationships, homes and families. We pray for children and families receiving help from Child and Adolescent Mental Health Services. We pray for children and adults traumatized by sexual, physical or emotional abuse. We pray for those who suffer mental ill health in old age, for those whose memories and faculties are taken from them by dementia, and for those who care for them.

Lord, in your mercy,
hear our prayer.

We pray for counsellors, psychotherapists, psychiatrists, clinical psychologists, nurses, occupational therapists, chaplains and all who care for people suffering from mental illness. We pray for members of therapeutic communities, mutual support groups and recovery colleges. We pray for charities and local church projects, devoted to the care and support of people with mental health problems. We pray for those who undertake research into mental disorders, seeking to relieve and prevent mental suffering. We pray for politicians, policy makers and managers who seek to plan, build and deliver better, more effective and more compassionate mental health services.

Lord, in your mercy,
hear our prayer.

Heavenly Father, we pray that, as Christ's body here on earth, and empowered by the Holy Spirit, we might bring healing and new life to those who suffer in mind and soul, both within our churches and in wider society. May we be bringers of forgiveness, kindness, faith, hope and love. Save us from shallow answers that add to the suffering of others. Help us to listen well. We pray that our churches may be places within which we welcome, nurture, encourage and include one another, and in which we do not tolerate stigma and prejudice. May we know your presence with us, may we find you in one another and may we be Christ for others.

Merciful Father,
accept these prayers for the sake of your Son, our Saviour, Jesus Christ.
Amen

Ingram Content Group UK Ltd.
Milton Keynes UK
UKHW020705230423
420621UK00009B/1150